Charles Darwin

For Gloria E. Bader – A human life is but a single wink in the inestimable expanse of evolutionary time; I am indeed fortunate to have shared most of that ephemeral wink with you.

Published by
REAKTION BOOKS LTD
Unit 32, Waterside
44–48 Wharf Road
London N1 7UX, UK
www.reaktionbooks.co.uk

First published 2021
Copyright © J. David Archibald 2021

Printed and bound in Great Britain by TJ Books Ltd, Padstow, Cornwall

A catalogue record for this book is available from the British Library

ISBN 978 1 78914 440 6

Contents

Preface 7

1 Few Memories of My Mother 11

2 Edinburgh Attempt, Cambridge Success 24

3 The Most Important Event in My Life 41

4 A New Scientific Career and a New Wife 67

5 A Momentous Move 86

6 Where Does He Do His Barnacles? 99

7 Lyell's Words Come True with a Vengeance 110

8 Reviews and Reactions 133

9 Bringing the 'Big Book' to Fruition 156

10 Teasing Plants and Tending Worms 169

11 Not the Least Afraid of Death 183

References 201

Bibliography 213

Acknowledgements 221

Photo Acknowledgements 223

Charles Darwin, *c.* 1855.

Preface

History is replete with serendipitous events. The history of science is no exception. In 1858 Charles Darwin was toiling away on his multi-volume work on the 'species question' – what today we know as evolution – as he had been doing off and on for the past twenty years. Then in June a letter and written essay arrived from islands in faraway Southeast Asia. The enclosed essay by Alfred Russel Wallace threatened to overturn the life's work of Darwin. Wallace had independently discovered descent with modification by means of natural selection. Although his vocabulary differed, Darwin realized that many of Wallace's arguments were so similar that they could serve as headings for chapters in Darwin's book. Darwin's friend and sometime mentor, the Scottish geologist Charles Lyell, had warned Darwin repeatedly that such an event was a very likely outcome. Interest in evolution was in the air.

The anonymously written book *Vestiges of the Natural History of Creation* had also appeared more than ten years earlier. Although publicly popular but scientifically panned, the book nevertheless primed the public and scientists for a more serious treatment of the topic of evolution. Darwin was beside himself anguishing over what to do regarding Wallace's letter and essay. Lyell and the English botanist Joseph Dalton Hooker came to the rescue with an honourable solution. The next month a joint paper by Wallace and Darwin would be presented at the Linnean Society meeting listing Darwin and Wallace as co-discoverers of evolution by means of natural selection. Darwin need not have worried. Wallace and Darwin's joint paper caused barely a ripple among those in the know.

Wallace had done us a favour. If he had not sent Darwin his letter and essay, Darwin probably would have dithered on for many years writing a ponderous multi-volume work that rather few people would have bothered to read. Instead, through that summer and into the next year Darwin toiled on a much shorter work that he wished to call an abstract in the title, but his publisher, John Murray, demurred as the volume would run to just over five hundred published pages. It included but one figure, a fold-out diagram showing a hypothetical evolutionary history. This book would not only turn the scientific community on its head, but would further erode the august place humans, especially white European males, had carved for themselves in God's creation.

Charles Darwin was not a polymath in the broader sense of someone whose breadth of knowledge spans many different disciplines. In the nineteenth century many natural historians such as Darwin displayed a broader scientific knowledge than is usual among twentieth- and twenty-first-century scientists. In Darwin's case this breadth was especially extensive, even more so than many of his contemporaries, and he made demonstrably important contributions in most of these fields. Rather obviously his crowning discovery, and still regarded as such today, is the primary driver of evolution – natural selection, the discovery of which he shared with Wallace. As a young man Darwin witnessed the stirrings of the recently energized sciences of geology and biology that were placing humans in a newly realized place in nature. Even his paternal grandfather Erasmus Darwin wrote poetry and prose imbued with the message of evolutionary change, writing in his 1794–6 *Zoonomia*, 'would it be too bold to imagine, that all warm-blooded animals have arisen from one living filament.'[1] Charles Darwin certainly could not know of his future in expanding well beyond his grandfather's ideas, demonstrating that evolution occurred and is occurring and that the rightful place of humans is within the natural world. In his autobiography he related that as a young man of just sixteen years old, his father castigated him for caring 'for nothing but shooting, dogs, and rat-catching' and said that he would 'be a disgrace to yourself and all your family'.[2] Fortunately for us, a finally relenting father's approval, the encouragement of a great mentor at the University of Cambridge, and the fortuitous opportunity to sail around the world in the pursuit of nature's deepest mysteries thrust Darwin onto the stage of human history and great scientific achievement.

By the time Darwin returned from the almost five-year voyage on the HMS *Beagle* in October 1836, he had convinced himself of the veracity of evolution mostly through the discovery of faunal succession (especially on continents such as Australia and South America), the geographical distribution of living plants and animals on the various continents and in the seas, and the rather peculiar kinds of plants and animals found on oceanic islands such as the Galápagos, far from the mainland. He began writing of his findings and musings in private notebooks in 1837, but at that time did not have a mechanism for evolutionary change. Within a year he had read the work of Thomas Robert Malthus, who wrote about how human populations would increase if not checked by famine, disease and war. Darwin realized that this applied to the natural realm as well, coining the term 'natural selection' to describe the winnowing of individuals within species in nature. Natural selection proved the force and check on population change and growth. It was not until more than twenty years later that Darwin published his findings in *On the Origin of Species*, and our perception of our place in nature would never be the same again. He provided not only the proof of evolution, but for the first time along with Wallace provided a viable evolutionary mechanism – natural selection.

Today we call it the theory of evolution by means of natural selection. It certainly is a theory in the sense that scientists use the word, but scientists also refer to the heliocentric theory of the solar system, the theory of gravity, and the theory that Earth is spherical. In the same way that we accept the fact that Earth circles the Sun, that apples fall from trees, and Earth is round, we also know it is a fact that life has evolved and continues to evolve.

1

Few Memories of My Mother

A large Georgian home stands on a rise above the River Severn just outside the town of Shrewsbury, in Shropshire, England. Today it houses the Valuation Office Agency, which as the name suggests values properties for the purpose of taxation. Built in 1800 and known then as the Mount House or The Mount, it was to play a much greater role in history than its present pedestrian use. It was the birthplace of Charles Robert Darwin on 12 February 1809, the co-discoverer of natural selection, the powerful mechanism that controls most evolutionary change. Darwin came from a family of considerable accomplishment well before he ever made indelible marks on biology and humans' perception of their place in nature.

Charles Darwin's paternal grandfather, Erasmus, was a well-known and well-respected physician, natural philosopher (precursor to scientist) and poet. He completed his undergraduate studies at the University of Cambridge and then his medical training at the University of Edinburgh, where his son Robert and his grandson Erasmus 'Ras', but not his other grandson Charles, completed their medical training. For more than fifty years Erasmus maintained a very lucrative medical practice in Lichfield in the West Midlands. Some of his writings clearly advocated a Lamarckian form of evolution, even before Lamarck, in which a parent acquires characteristics during its lifetime through use or disuse that are in turn passed along to its offspring. His primary works advocating this theory included his *Zoonomia* (1794–6)

The Mount, Shrewsbury, birthplace of Charles Robert Darwin.

and *The Temple of Nature* (1803). His grandson Charles Darwin certainly knew of his grandfather's genteel dabbling in evolution, acknowledging him in his historical sketch in later editions of *On the Origin of Species* as a precursor to his own evolutionary theorizing. The two never met; Erasmus died seven years before Charles was born.

Erasmus helped found the Lunar Society, an influential group in the region around Birmingham, England, whose members were natural philosophers, intellectuals and early industrialists. The name of the society derived from the group meeting each month on the full moon, allowing them better light for travelling at night. He also was a friend and correspondent of Benjamin Franklin during Franklin's second mission to England between 1764 and 1775 before the War of Independence. Erasmus married twice and fathered at least fourteen children. His children include two illegitimate daughters by an employee, with rumours that he fathered yet another child by a married woman. Erasmus was a vocal advocate

Erasmus Darwin, paternal grandfather of Charles Darwin, *c.* 1803.

of formal, school-based education for women, even though his behaviour towards women might seem less than honourable.

In the 1790s Erasmus was in his mid-sixties with a stellar reputation as a physician and as a poet known around the country. Patients came from as far away as London. One client in particular, with a cousin who worked as a governess in the Royal Household, raved about her care from Erasmus Darwin. When word reached King George III of the governess's medical treatment he asked if

Erasmus might not come to London, serving as the king's physician. Erasmus demurred, as he was already, owing to his increasing age, shrinking his practice and reducing his visits to local patients.

Robert Waring Darwin, father of Charles Robert Darwin, was the fourth child of Erasmus and Mary Darwin. He received small inheritances from his father and various family members which he used wisely, including construction of The Mount in 1800. He received rents from buildings he owned in Shrewsbury and invested in ventures such as the London to Holyhead Road and the

Robert Waring Darwin, father of Charles Darwin, 1839.

Trent and Mersey Canal, both proving successful projects amid the industrialization of England. Like his father Erasmus, Robert was a very successful physician who showed great care to his patients. Also, and even more so than his father Erasmus, although 188 centimetres (6 ft 2 in.) tall, Robert became very corpulent, at 150 kilograms (330 lb) when he last allowed himself to be weighed. As other physicians of the time, especially those outside of large cities, Robert regularly used a gig, the favoured two-wheeled one-horse carriage, to visit patients in their homes. Because of his size, his coachman was sometimes obliged to test the floorboards in the homes, especially of poorer patients, lest they not support his weight. Probably with a loving tongue-in-cheek, Charles later in life referred to his father as 'the largest man I ever knew'. Although putting on a bit of extra weight in middle age, the 6-foot-tall Charles did not follow in his father and grandfather's girth, probably owing to the debilitating stomach ailments he suffered during much of his adulthood.

Charles Darwin's maternal grandfather Josiah Wedgwood was also a member of the Lunar Society and friend of Erasmus Darwin. In 1759 Josiah founded what became Josiah Wedgwood & Sons, the famous pottery manufacturer. He was known for his systematic experimentation to improve his products. He produced high-quality items for the expensive tastes of high-society clients and also made less expensive versions to appeal to a broader, less sophisticated market.

Both the Darwins and Wedgwoods were staunchly anti-slavery, which Charles, through his upbringing, certainly also learned to be. Josiah Wedgwood mass-produced the small medallion that would become famous for its motto 'Am I Not a Man and a Brother?', below a pleading, shackled African man. The parliamentary leader for the abolition of slavery, William Wilberforce, and Josiah Wedgwood corresponded numerous times regarding this national issue. Wilberforce even visited the Wedgwood home Etruria Hall.

Josiah Wedgwood, maternal grandfather of Charles Darwin.

In a twist of fate, many years later Wedgwood's grandson Charles and Wilberforce's son Samuel, later a bishop, became bitter enemies over Darwin's evolutionary work. Samuel Wilberforce was probably a key player in denying Darwin a knighthood.

Susannah 'Sukey' Wedgwood, mother of Charles Robert Darwin, was the first child of Josiah and Sarah Wedgwood. She is described as popular, spirited and intelligent, and she and her father were particularly close. She was educated both at home and at a boarding school. The 29-year-old Robert Waring Darwin and 28-year-old Susannah were engaged in 1794 and married in 1796. Robert's father Erasmus and Susannah's father Josiah had been friends for many years, so the match of the two young people was not a surprise.

Robert and Susannah had six children – Marianne (1798), Caroline Sarah (1800), Susan Elizabeth (1803), Erasmus Alvey 'Ras' (1804), who was named after their paternal grandfather, Charles (1809), and the youngest, Emily Catherine (1810). A charming chalk portrait of Emily Catherine and Charles shows Charles clutching in his interlocked fingers a pot probably containing the perennial *Lachenalia*, portending his future as a naturalist. Only the four older Darwin children had many memories of their mother, because Susannah died aged 52 of an undetermined stomach ailment, possibly stomach cancer or a greatly inflamed ulcer. Only eight years old when she died, Charles would later recall

Anti-slavery medallion with the inscription 'Am I not a man and a brother?', produced by Josiah Wedgwood, after 1786, terracotta on basalt.

little more than his mother's deathbed and her black gown. After their mother's death, Charles and his sister Emily Catherine, who was only a year younger than Charles, were cared for by his older sisters. Charles's connection to his maternal relatives would prove a powerful force even after his mother's death, because her brother Josiah Wedgwood II and his large family of nine children lived some 48 kilometres (30 mi.) to the northeast at Maer Hall, a place where Charles often visited and stayed. What would prove even more profound in Darwin's life was his 1839 marriage to his first cousin, Emma, the youngest of the Wedgwood children – but that was still more than twenty years in the future.

Most of the Darwin and Wedgwood families, including Charles's grandfathers Erasmus Darwin and Josiah Wedgwood, practised Unitarianism, considered then even more so than now as

Peter Paillou the Younger, *Susannah Wedgwood, Mother of Charles Darwin*, 1793, watercolour on ivory.

Ellen Sharples, *Charles and Catherine Darwin*, 1816, chalk drawing.

quite liberal, rejecting doctrines believed by most other Christian denominations such as the Bible's infallibility, original sin and predestination. A phrase common in both families and often attributed to Charles's grandfather Erasmus called Unitarianism 'a featherbed to catch a falling Christian'. Some, such as Charles's mother Susannah, attended the Unitarian Chapel on High Street in Shrewsbury, but also kept a firm foot in the Church of England; Susannah had Charles baptized at St Chad's, Shrewsbury, in 1809. Susannah as well as Charles's father Robert and sisters Emily Catherine and Susan are buried there. As a very young boy Charles attended services at St Chad's with his mother and then after her death he attended the High Street Unitarian Chapel with his older sisters. Both Charles and his older brother Ras were christened in the Church of England, knowing full well that if they wished to attend the universities of Oxford or Cambridge, membership of the Church of England was a prerequisite along with being a white male and subscribing to the Thirty-nine Articles of Religion, the statements of doctrines and practices of the Church.

The young Darwin could never be called a studious child. From a very early age, to the consternation of his father, the rambunctious boy already showed a strong love of the outdoors and all of nature's treasures. He could not be blamed for this, because the surroundings of The Mount afforded him every opportunity to see nature up close. He loved to collect all manner of things, especially natural objects. This was in part done to stand out as a boy in a home dominated by older sisters and also resulted from his parents providing ample opportunity to stoke his interests, a child-rearing method he would foster with his own family. When he wanted to begin collecting insects, he followed an older sister's advice to collect only those that were already dead, because it was not kind to kill insects purely for his collection. The Mount also boasted a well-appointed greenhouse with exotic plants in which a young boy could sequester himself. The family kept a variety of tame, fancy pigeons that certainly caught the budding young naturalist's eye – this interest would be rekindled in later life when Charles bred pigeons for studies of variation in domesticated species. He preferred nature to the confines of a classroom and the stodginess of a Midlands education.

Darwin's father possessed a significant library that included many volumes dealing with the natural world. Although no scholar by temperament, the young Darwin no doubt found books there that whetted his appetite for the natural sciences. In his autobiography many years later he singled out Gilbert White's

The Natural History and Antiquities of Selborne (1789). As he related in his autobiography, White's book brought him much pleasure in opening up to him the world of bird-watching, including learning how to take notes on their habits.[1] He also related how his older brother Ras introduced him to a boyish enthusiasm for chemistry. Ras had assembled a decent laboratory in the garden tool-house, including apparatus for doing experiments. He allowed the much younger Charles to serve as his assistant in creating all manner of gases and compounds. He also recounted that he read various chemistry books to acquaint himself with how the processes were to take place. This for him was his true education, not the stifling strictures of the formal classroom. News of his chemistry exploits eventually reached his teasing Shrewsbury classmates, who christened him 'Gas'. It also reinforced his disdain for formal education when the headmaster called such pursuits a waste of time.[2]

Darwin had begun his formal schooling at a day school in Shrewsbury run by the Unitarians and associated with the Unitarian Chapel that he had sometimes attended with his mother. After his mother's death Charles joined Ras in 1818 at the Anglican Shrewsbury School run by Samuel Butler where he remained until 1825, when he was sixteen. This Samuel Butler was the grandfather of the eponymous writer who authored the popular novel *Erewhon* about a society incongruously combining utopian and dystopian aspects. The writer was the same man who would later criticize Darwin's ideas on evolution, accusing Darwin of plagiarizing the theoretical work of others, including his own paternal grandfather Erasmus. Charles was a boarder at Dr Butler's school, although his home was only a mile away. As he recounted, being a fleet-footed runner, he often ran from school to home then back again in between his scholastic obligations, making sure to arrive back at school before being locked in at night.[3]

Charles held Butler's school in low regard, recalling his time there as an educational blank, because it taught only classical topics

The old Shrewsbury School, Shrewsbury.

such as ancient geography and history. Truth be told, although
the school was no doubt dull for an active and mischievous boy,
Charles was the first to admit that throughout his academic career
he never much cared for classroom-based education. As Darwin
related in his autobiography, he was considered quite an ordinary
student, rather below average in his intellect. The famous quote he
attributed to his father – 'You care for nothing but shooting, dogs,
and rat-catching, and you will be a disgrace to yourself and all your
family' – bears repeating as it once again informs us of the life of
nature and science that Darwin was to lead.[4] He knew his father
loved him dearly, but his kindness was sorely tried by his teenage
son's wilful disregard for formal education.

In 1825 Robert withdrew the sixteen-year-old Charles from Shrewsbury School and arranged for him to enter the University of Edinburgh. In a diligent attempt to prepare for attending school at Edinburgh with the intention of becoming a doctor like his grandfather, father and brother, that summer Darwin began attending to the medical needs of poor people, especially children and women, in Shrewsbury. At one point he reports taking care of as many as a dozen patients. He dutifully wrote as complete an account of his cases as possible, noting all symptoms. He would consult with his father, who suggested any further course of action including any medicines to be given, which Darwin then prescribed for his patients.

Darwin felt a keen interest in his medical work, but it must be remembered that he was only sixteen years old that summer. His father encouraged him, noting that he would be successful as a physician.[5] What began as a summer of youthful exuberance for medicine would soon run headlong into the reality of academic and clinical hoops Darwin would need to leap through on the way to becoming a physician. A few short months later he was to join his brother, Ras, in Edinburgh. It was the first time he had been away from home, plonked down in the middle of a teeming nineteenth-century Scottish city for which he was ill prepared.

2

Edinburgh Attempt, Cambridge Success

In October 1825 Charles joined Ras at the University of Edinburgh to pursue a medical career, following in the footsteps of their paternal grandfather and father before them. Ras was in Edinburgh doing his required one-year hospital stint away from Christ's College, University of Cambridge, on his way to becoming a physician. A new if not wholly successful academic experience awaited Charles at Edinburgh.

Charles rented rooms from Mrs Mackay with his brother Ras at 11 Lothian Street in the Old Town of Edinburgh in which he remained during his brother's year in Edinburgh, the second year moving a short distance away to smaller quarters, also on Lothian Street. Charles described his and his brother's accommodations on the fourth floor, which consisted of two bedrooms and a sitting room, as light and airy, rare commodities in Edinburgh, where more often than not rooms lacked both.[1]

By the time Charles arrived in Edinburgh the city had cast itself as the 'Athens of the North'. Perhaps a pretentious moniker, nevertheless the city could boast some grand architecture as well as a rightful claim as a major centre of economics, philosophy and medicine. It had been home to a litany of famous men in the previous century such as the chemist Joseph Black, the biographer James Boswell, the philosopher David Hume, the geologist James Hutton and the economist Adam Smith.

Generally impressed with the grandeur of the city's buildings but less so with urban squalor, Charles and Ras were also disappointed with some of the yet to be completed university buildings started many years earlier when their father was a student. In the end this mattered little to Charles as he maintained his lackadaisical pursuit of his formal education, notably his general loathing for lectures, which he recalled as being intolerably dull. Lectures constituted most of his formal education at Edinburgh. Some of his lecturers were famous in their own right but this did not stop him from savaging them many years later in his autobiography. Early morning lectures by Andrew Duncan, the younger, professor of *materia medica*, on the history and uses of pharmaceutical substances, were a truly fearful experience to remember. Darwin described the human anatomy lectures of the renowned anatomist Alexander Monro (tertius), misspelled as Munro, as being as dull as the man. Monro gained the 'tertius' epithet because he followed his grandfather and father of the same name in this same position teaching anatomy. One exception to numbing lectures was the chemistry professor Thomas Charles Hope, who entertained his audience. Hope introduced the teenager to what became known as the Plutonist or Vulcanist theory of geology, arguing that not all rocks are deposited as precipitates from water, but rather some are formed through heat in the earth such as through volcanic activity. A variant of this would soon prove to be the prevailing geological theory.[2]

The clinical and especially the surgical presentations Darwin was required to attend as a medical student finally turned him away from medicine. Many of the cases he observed on clinical rounds, which he dutifully attended, distressed him greatly. This was the case even though the summer before arriving at Edinburgh he had gladly accompanied his father on patient rounds in the Shrewsbury region. The final straw ending his medical career came when he attended two difficult surgeries that were done before

Old College, historic heart of the University of Edinburgh, 1840.

the advent of general anaesthesia. He described rushing from the operating theatre during surgery on a child, never to return.

During his time in Edinburgh Darwin regretted not having experienced actual dissection instruction, which unlike the then brutal quality of surgery would have been extremely beneficial in his later scientific pursuits. He did, however, learn what would later prove to be the invaluable art of skinning and preparing bird specimens from the former slave John Edmonstone (or Edmonston).[3] Edmonstone enthralled the young Darwin with tales of tropical South America, where he had been enslaved from birth. Edmonstone had learned his skills from the English naturalist and conservationist Charles Waterton while still a slave on a plantation in present-day Guyana. Edmonstone came to Glasgow with his former owner and later moved to Edinburgh where he taught taxidermy to the students, including Darwin, at 37 Lothian Street – the same street upon which Darwin lived.

Darwin never mentioned Edmonstone by name, only referring to him in an 1826 letter to his sister Susan Elizabeth as the 'blackamoor' who would teach him how to stuff birds.[4] 'Blackamoor' was a somewhat contemptuous name for those of black African descent. Whereas Darwin probably gave little thought to referring to this man in such a dismissive manner, he learned from his paternal family and especially his maternal one of the evils of slavery. Darwin inherited the anti-slavery ethos of both the Darwin and Wedgwood families. The Slave Trade Act of 1807 outlawed the slave trade just before Darwin was born, but it would not be until 1833 that slavery was outlawed in all colonies of the British Empire.

When his brother Ras left Edinburgh after his one-year academic stay to return to Cambridge, Darwin began to expand his social and academic horizons. It is from these associations that we can see him begin to transform from a hunter, sportsman and collector into a budding scientific naturalist. At this time, he was also pointedly confronted with the evolutionary writings of his grandfather Erasmus, whom he had read but never really digested or discussed with others. This was to change.

Darwin became acquainted with a number of young men who shared scientific theories and ideas. The young licensed surgeon and later geologist William Francis Ainsworth introduced him to what became known as the Neptunian theory of geology which argued that all rocks are deposited as precipitates or insoluble substances emerging from water, in contrast to the Plutonist theory Darwin had learned of in Thomas Charles Hope's lectures. The geology professor Robert Jameson also presented the Neptunian theory to Darwin in his second year, but Jameson's lectures on the topic were so dull that Darwin recalled many years afterwards how the professor was an 'old brown, dry stick', a view shared by others.[5] Never mind that Neptunian theory would soon lose scientific favour to the Plutonist theory. Hope's lectures on the Plutonist theory helped spark Darwin's interest in geology, which would prove a profound part of his later scientific endeavours.

Jameson's only real effect on Darwin was in solidifying the student's determination that, as long as he should live, he would never read a book on geology. Yet we know this would not continue to be the case. What sparked Darwin's interest was seeing the real thing in the field and pondering why it was the way it was. This extended to those who could show him the wonders of the natural world such as William MacGillivray, then conservator of the Royal College of Surgeons Museum, Edinburgh, whom Darwin held in esteem. He was very kind to Darwin and helped to foster Darwin's interest in natural history, even though, as Darwin related, MacGillivray did not project the demeanour of a gentleman – an opinion reflecting Darwin's acceptance of the English class system. MacGillivray even gifted Darwin rare shells because of Darwin's passing interest in marine molluscs. Darwin was impressed that MacGillivray went on to publish a book, *A History of British Birds*.[6]

This encounter, which Darwin related later in life, shows that he was beginning to emerge from the bubble of the English upper middle class, appreciating what he could learn from others who were not of his social status. He related a similar story about an older man in Shrewsbury, a Mr Cotton, who imparted to Darwin his knowledge of the local geology. Cotton was especially intrigued by a local geological landmark – a large erratic boulder called the Bellstone, which can still be observed in Shrewsbury today. He related to Darwin that there were no rocks like this nearer than Scotland or Cumberland in northwest England and that the world would end before anyone could figure out its origin.[7] It would be some years later that Darwin learned that continental glaciers had deposited such massive stones far to the south of their native rocks.

Other influential people in Darwin's life in Edinburgh included fellow medical students such as John Coldstream. He was one of five nominators of Darwin to the Plinian Society, a club for undergraduates at the University of Edinburgh interested in natural history which was started by Jameson, which Darwin joined in the autumn of 1826. The club made field excursions to the Edinburgh countryside, read and discussed papers on natural science, and even presented papers on their own work. Charles accompanied Ainsworth, noted earlier, as well as others on expeditions to the nearby Firth of Forth, north of Edinburgh, to study and collect marine life. The leader for most trips was the medically trained zoologist Robert Edmond Grant, who was studying the local marine life. Darwin's relationship with Grant proved to be troubled on both sides for several reasons. Grant was a free-thinker, materialist, and radical in his political views. He knew of and quoted Erasmus Darwin's clearly expressed evolutionary ideas espoused in *Zoonomia* as well as knowing scientists with similar ideas in France. Even though he had himself read his grandfather's work, Darwin was taken aback by Grant's overly enthusiastic admiration of evolutionists such as Lamarck and Erasmus Darwin. This proved too much for the young and still religiously inclined Darwin.

On excursions to the Firth of Forth Darwin recovered a number of specimens that were new to science. One discovery was what we now know to be the larvae of the bryozoan *Flustra*, which by means of cilia are capable of movement. Another discovery was of small globular bodies that were then believed to be the early life stages of a brown alga but in fact were egg cases of a leech. Certainly, as an eighteen-year-old budding scientist Darwin failed to realize that he should have shared more fully with Grant his discoveries done under Grant's aegis. Grant in turn was remiss in reporting Darwin's two discoveries as his own. He barely acknowledged that Darwin had discovered what we now know to be leech egg cases.

In extant records at the University of Edinburgh, minutes of the Plinian Society show that on 27 March 1827 Darwin, at only eighteen years old, gave his first scientific presentation concerning the bryozoan *Flustra*, a marine colonial organism. As it turned out, Grant had already reported on this find without crediting Darwin.[8] This proved an important object lesson for the young Darwin which he strove to adhere to for the remainder of his life – he would give proper credit to the rightful discoverer of scientific facts and proposers of scientific theories. This dilemma would become tantamount in his mind when 31 years later he faced the possibility that credit for his theory of descent with modification by means of natural selection might be claimed by the much younger Alfred Russel Wallace.

After completing his second and what would be his last year at Edinburgh in 1827 Darwin travelled around Scotland, also visiting Ireland. He continued his wanderlust by accompanying his uncle Josiah Wedgwood II and his sister Caroline to Paris. These would prove to be his only trips outside of Great Britain, with the amazing exception that in the near future he would sail around the globe for almost five years. Darwin continued his devil-may-care existence in summer and into early autumn 1827, notably hunting near Shrewsbury on the estate of William Mostyn Owen. Here he met his first love, Fanny, daughter of William and sister of a school friend also named William Owen. During that summer Darwin spent considerable time with Fanny pursuing mutual interests in riding, shooting and playing billiards, and flirting. Her interest in such activities as shooting surprised and apparently pleased Darwin, as did her coquettishness and teasing.[9] Their relationship would continue off and on over the next few years.

With Darwin not returning to Edinburgh, it became clear to his father that his youngest son was not destined to follow the family tradition in medicine. What he would instead do became the issue. Darwin certainly could not continue to lead an idle sporting life as he clearly was doing upon leaving Edinburgh, especially if Robert Darwin had any say in the matter, and of course he did. It must be realized that many modern career paths simply did not exist in the early nineteenth century, notably for someone such as Charles Darwin, whose scientific pursuits were avocational. One possible path was for Darwin to finish his undergraduate degree with the aim of then continuing his studies and eventually becoming a clergyman. There was talk of how he could then settle into a small country parish with enough remaining time to pursue his growing avocational interest in natural history.

The decision came for Darwin to head to the University of Cambridge to complete his undergraduate degree, but it would mean a major shift in emphasis. He would be switching from coursework in medicine that he had attempted but failed to learn at Edinburgh to a much more classically oriented course of study at Cambridge. He was not prepared and thus did not begin Cambridge in the autumn of 1827. Rather, a tutor was employed in the closing months of that year to refresh him in the classical studies and language that he had not done since before attending Edinburgh and would now need at Cambridge.

Darwin arrived in the winter of 1828 at Christ's College, Cambridge, the same college where his brother Ras had studied medicine. Darwin later assessed the three years he spent at Cambridge as being as much of an academic waste of time as his formal coursework at Edinburgh. He complained about the apparent uselessness of learning algebra and his lack of attentiveness in the classics beyond a few compulsory lectures, yet in March 1830, with just a few months study, he easily passed the 'Little Go', the examination then required of Cambridge undergraduates in the year before their graduation.[10] In early 1831, his last year, he once again studied enough to pass his final exams in classics and mathematics. He graduated without honours, although managed to rank in tenth place out of 178 students in spring 1831.

Unlike for classics and mathematics, Darwin did apply himself to the required study of William Paley's influential book *Principles of Moral and Political Philosophy*, first published in 1785. Uncharacteristically for Darwin, he went further, reading Paley's *Natural Theology or Evidences of the Existence and Attributes of the Deity* (1802), which although not a required text greatly

Christ's College, University of Cambridge, 1838, engraving by J. Le Keux.

impressed Darwin with its well-considered line of theological argumentation, including the famous teleological watchmaker argument for God's existence.[11] The tenor of the book followed the natural theology tradition dating back to ancient philosophers. It provided arguments for the goodness and existence of God. Paley's arguments were a series of examples comparing the natural world and man-made objects, such as finely tuned joints in animals versus man-made ball-and-socket joints or the human eye versus a telescope. The most famous is the watchmaker analogy in which he argues that just as the complexity of a watch calls out for the existence of a watchmaker so the complexities in nature point to a divine maker. Such arguments certainly impressed the young and still quite impressionable Darwin.

An additional but unproven connection between Darwin and Paley purports that they may have occupied the same rooms at Christ's College, although some seventy years apart. Although it is a great story there is little but college lore to support it. To paraphrase the philosopher, astronomer and fellow iconoclast Giordano Bruno – burnt at the stake in 1600 in Rome for advocating an infinite universe – even if the Darwin–Paley connection is not true, it makes a good story.[12] Nevertheless, portraits of Paley and Darwin face each other in the hall of Christ's College.

At Cambridge just as at Edinburgh, Darwin did learn a great deal, but most of the knowledge obtained came through extra-curricular activities that continued to encourage his overriding interest in nature. One pursuit that consumed him was the *au courant* Victorian passion of collecting beetles. In his autobiography, he related his sometimes-misplaced zeal in beetle-collecting. As he tells the story, he found two rare beetles under some tree bark and placed one in each hand. Upon spying a third new form he popped one in his mouth to free up a hand to be greeted by an acrid fluid burning his tongue, causing him to spit it out, resulting in the loss of the other two specimens, too.[13] Darwin's acumen at beetling earned him several caricatures drawn by Cambridge friend and fellow beetle collector Albert Way. The figures show Darwin astride a beetle labelled as his 'hobby', a play on words referring to his hobby of collecting beetles and to the toy hobby horse. It also earned him the attention of the entomologist

James Francis Stephens. Stephens used some of Darwin's specimens in at least five of the earlier volumes in his 1828–46 *Illustrations of British Entomology*, citing him as 'captured by C. Darwin, Esq.' and bringing delight at seeing his name in print, something that Grant had failed to do when Darwin worked with him in Edinburgh.

This passion soon found direction and purpose. He was very fortunate to come under the tutelage of Professor John Stevens Henslow, who through fieldwork and guidance honed Darwin's skill in observation of the natural world, turning him from a collector of beetles into an aspiring naturalist when he finished university early in 1831. One cannot understate the importance of Henslow in Darwin's scientific upbringing and the future course his life would take. By the time Darwin arrived at Cambridge in 1828, Henslow had been professor of botany for almost three years. Before that he had been professor of mineralogy for three years, appointed at the young age of 26. A major influence on Henslow had been Adam Sedgwick, who was professor of geology at Cambridge for his entire career. Henslow learned geology from accompanying Sedgwick on field excursions around England, thus it was natural for him to

Caricature of Darwin riding his 'hobby, a beetle', by Albert Way (1805–1874).

John Stevens Henslow, Darwin's mentor at the University of Cambridge, 1849.

accept the position of professor of mineralogy, yet when the botany professorship became vacant in 1825, he was keen to accept, as botany was his true passion. Sedgwick and Henslow also took holy orders in the Church of England in addition to their professorial duties, not an uncommon practice for scientifically minded men of the time. In the case of Henslow, in addition to his professorships at Cambridge he held various ecclesiastical positions.

Darwin certainly knew of Henslow, but it was his second cousin, fellow beetle collector and lifelong correspondent William Darwin

Fox who formally introduced the two. Thereafter Darwin attended lectures by Henslow and went to weekly gatherings Henslow held at his home. Darwin already had the naturalist bug, but it was Henslow who began to redirect this into a more systematic approach, a process that had begun in Edinburgh. Darwin accompanied Henslow on natural history collecting expeditions around the Cambridge countryside, and these trips became the beginning of Darwin's training in field geology. Greatly respecting Henslow and knowing that he had been trained by Sedgwick caused Darwin to regret his quite irregular attendance at Sedgwick's Cambridge lectures. Inspired by Henslow's mentoring and the accounts of the Prussian naturalist Alexander von Humboldt, Darwin and like-minded Cambridge friends hatched a plan to visit Tenerife in the Canary Islands after Darwin's graduation in April 1831. This meant that Darwin would now need to take his geological education more seriously. Plans for the Tenerife trip, however, were dashed upon his return to his family home in Shrewsbury when he learned that one of the participants, his friend Marmaduke Ramsay, had died suddenly.

In the summer of 1831 after the Tenerife plans fell through, Henslow helped arrange for Darwin to do geological fieldwork in Wales with Adam Sedgwick. This would be a challenge for Darwin to put his newly learned field geology skills to the test as well as learning new skills from Sedgwick. Although Darwin probably had not attended Sedgwick's geology lectures, they had met, most likely at one of Henslow's soirées. The excursion to Wales was to be quite short, only a week or so. In preparation, the geological neophyte acquired a clinometer for measuring slope angles and elevations. Darwin practised with the instrument near The Mount in Shrewsbury. He produced a crude geological map of parts of the county, bringing him to the realization that such endeavours required more skill than he possessed. In early August 1831, Sedgwick arrived at The Mount, spending several nights before

Darwin and he departed for Wales. Having such a distinguished Cambridge professor staying at The Mount was a momentous event for the young Darwin. The field project in northern Wales, just west of Shropshire, that Sedgwick had undertaken entailed examining rocks containing some of the then earliest-known fossils on Earth.

In an attempt to impress Sedgwick while at The Mount, Darwin related how a labourer recovered a tropical shell in a local gravel pit. Sedgwick found the story amusing, indicating that if true, it would overturn the known geology in the region. Sedgwick indicated that the shell must have been thrown into the pit by a passer-by. He stressed how one must gather supportive data before drawing general conclusions. A piece of evidence such as the single shell cannot negate all other previously known information. Darwin later related how this exchange made him realize that facts must be grouped together so that we might draw more general conclusions from them.[14] Not only had he learned the lesson of gathering as much data as possible before presenting a theory, but Darwin also learned to keep close counsel before going public with such theories – an important lesson he kept in mind with his later work on evolutionary theory.

One goal of the trip was to trace the geographic extent of the assemblage of rocks known as the Old Red Sandstone, a task with which Darwin was to help. Sedgwick had examined exposures of the Old Red Sandstone previously presented in the 1819 Greenough geological map of England and Wales. Darwin purchased a small-format version of the map to bring on the excursion. Darwin learned a tremendous amount about geological fieldwork from Sedgwick in the short time that they travelled together. Sedgwick explained to Darwin about the corals that composed these limestone beds, showed him the caves at Cefn where vertebrate fossils occurred, and uncovered a rhinoceros tooth. Darwin learned how to use overlying vegetation to identify underlying rocks, how to measure the dip of the geological strata, and how to properly draw geological maps and stratigraphic sections. Sedgwick also helped Darwin build his confidence by directing him to measure along an exposure by himself to determine the extent of the Old Red Sandstone that supposedly occurred there. Darwin could find no trace of the unit in the area he examined. Sedgwick was pleased by the thoughtful independence shown by Darwin. Darwin wrote to Henslow expressing his gratitude for what Sedgwick had taught him. Although still inexperienced as a geologist, this work provided him with the confidence and training that would stand him in good stead for the next, far grander, experience that was very soon to present itself.

A letter arrived for Henslow in summer 1831 inviting him to sail for two years aboard the surveying vessel HMS *Beagle*, ostensibly as a naturalist and probably a companion of equal social standing to the captain. Although others had probably turned down the offer and Henslow was sorely tempted to accept, his professional and familial responsibilities precluded him from accepting the role. Instead, he knew that although still an untested naturalist, as a recently minted Cambridge graduate Darwin would be an excellent choice. He forwarded his recommendation for Darwin to be recruited as the naturalist and companion to Robert FitzRoy, the commander of HMS *Beagle*. Just over three years older than Darwin, FitzRoy had in 1828 assumed command of the first South American expedition of the *Beagle* following the suicide of its commanding officer Pringle Stokes. This second voyage would be commanded by FitzRoy from the start.

When Charles approached his father about accepting the offer, the response was predictably negative. Robert could see no benefit and any number of disincentives of accepting such an offer, especially as Charles appeared to be no closer to settling on a suitable profession. As this was an unpaid position, Robert also would need to support his son while on the voyage. Robert did not flatly refuse but challenged Charles to find any man with

Robert FitzRoy, commander of the second voyage of HMS *Beagle*, c. 1835.

common sense who could put forth cogent arguments as to why Charles should accept. Despondent, he rode to Maer Hall to visit the Wedgwoods. While there he had occasion to tell his uncle Josiah 'Jos' about the potential opportunity to sail aboard the *Beagle* and the flat refusal of his father, except if he could find a man of sound reason who thought the trip a good idea. He found such a man in his uncle, who rode back to The Mount with his nephew to persuade his brother-in-law Robert that such an undertaking was indeed a worthwhile endeavour, although admittedly arduous, dangerous and long.

When he applied for the position, FitzRoy informed Darwin that he had offered the position to another individual. Later, FitzRoy admitted that he had invented this other person as an excuse in case he found Darwin unsuitable. FitzRoy offered Darwin the job after their early September 1831 meeting. Even then, according to Darwin, FitzRoy had some doubts about him because he had the wrong shaped nose.[15] This was based on FitzRoy's belief in the then *au courant* pseudoscience of phrenology that claimed to know a

William Owen, *Josiah Wedgwood II*, n.d., oil on canvas.

person's mental abililties and character based upon the shape and aspects of their head. The supposedly two-year expedition would be quite long enough for Darwin, and he was thrilled that FitzRoy had accepted him for the voyage, wrong nose or not, but of course he had no idea that two years would stretch to almost five before his return to England.

3

The Most Important Event in My Life

After some delays, HMS *Beagle* departed the environs of
Plymouth, England, on 27 December 1831 under the command
of Robert FitzRoy to begin its second expedition. Second and
third in command were lieutenants John Clements Wickham
and Bartholomew James Sulivan, the former having served with
FitzRoy on *Beagle*'s first voyage. This second voyage continued the
hydrographic survey of the southern coasts of South America for the
Admiralty begun during its first voyage in 1826–30. Hydrographic
surveys entailed the measurement and description of natural and
man-made features encountered in the sea during a ship's journey.
They provided important data to aid both commercial and military
interests for this nation that so dominated the seas. The ship relied
on 22 of the newest marine chronometers to help establish correct
longitudinal readings, essential in determining one's position. Even
with the undoubted importance of this surveying voyage, it would
have sunk into historical oblivion except for the presence of Charles
Darwin, whose later writings insured HMS *Beagle* a place in history.
Darwin later regarded his time on the *Beagle* as the most important
'event' in his life – never mind that this was no mere event.[1]
Although slated to take two or perhaps three years it extended to
almost five, a fifth of this young man's life.

Estimates vary, but aboard at various times were between 68
and 76 people, most as naval personnel. Among the exceptions
were a few people classed as supernumeraries, those who had

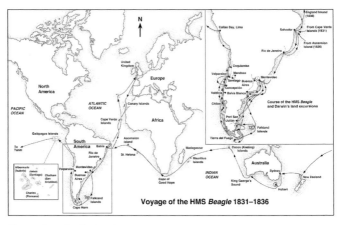

Voyage of HMS *Beagle*, 1831–6.

no official capacity as naval personnel. These included the artist and draughtsman Augustus Earle, the instrument maker George James Stebbing who maintained the 22 marine chronometers, three Fuegians taken as captives on the first *Beagle* voyage who were to be returned to Tierra del Fuego along with the missionary Richard Matthews, and finally the 22-year-old Darwin. As a recent Cambridge graduate he assumed the unofficial role of geologist/naturalist and companion of the captain but became official in this capacity when the ship's surgeon Robert McCormick left in a huff after a few months because his official role of naturalist, usually assumed by the ship's surgeon, had been usurped by this upstart. In return, Darwin did not hold McCormick in high regard; he found his scientific approaches antiquated and went as far as calling him an ass in a letter to Henslow.[2] Darwin was the social equal of the captain, and the only one who regularly dined with him. His elevated position did not go unnoticed by the crew, who at first simply called him 'sir', but within a matter of months as he settled into the ship's routine he became known to all as 'Philos' because FitzRoy began referring to him as the ship's philosopher.

Before the *Beagle* departed, FitzRoy presented Darwin with the first of what would become the three-volume *Principles of Geology* by Charles Lyell. Darwin acquired the other two volumes during stops on the voyage. Darwin also received before he sailed a bound copy of Alexander von Humboldt's *Personal Narrative*, probably a gift from Henslow. These were well-received as Lyell and Humboldt were two of Darwin's scientific idols: Lyell for promoting the concept of uniformitarianism, which among other things argued that present-day geological processes had also operated in the past, and Humboldt for his meticulous scientific exploration and reporting of the natural world in northern South America. During the voyage Darwin cited and quoted both men extensively in his various diaries and notebooks, indicating the profound influence they had on his thinking.[3] In addition to the books by Lyell and Humboldt, the *Beagle* boasted a library of more than four hundred volumes stored in the cramped poop cabin, also the chart room, at the stern of the vessel. Although dominated by books on travel, voyages and natural history that proved invaluable to Darwin there was also some literature. In particular Darwin enjoyed lounging on the sofa in the captain's cabin with a small, compact edition of Milton's *Paradise Lost*, sometimes his only respite from his perpetual sea-sickness.

Darwin shared this cabin *cum* library/chart room/laboratory, barely 3 × 4 metres (10 × 13 ft), with the assistant surveyor John Lort Stokes – no relation to Pringle Stokes, who was captain of the *Beagle* on the first expedition. The room was dominated by a chart table measuring some 1.8 metres (6 ft) in its greatest dimension above which they would stretch their hammocks. It also served as Darwin's makeshift laboratory while he was aboard ship. From here he prepared crates of specimens to be shipped back from various ports to England destined for Henslow, who acted as his receiving agent. Darwin could be happy that during its refitting for the second voyage FitzRoy had the upper deck on the aft portion of the *Beagle* raised 20 centimetres (8 in.) as well as adding a skylight, certainly making the snug accommodations for Darwin ever so slightly less snug. But as if one hand giveth and the other taketh away, the newly installed mizzen-mast drove its 25-centimetre (10 in.) diameter bulk at an angle through the front of this small cabin.

The *Beagle*'s first landfall was to be at Tenerife in the Canary Islands in January 1832. Darwin was excited not only because it would be his first port of call on the voyage, but because the planned trip there the previous summer had been dashed with the death of one of the participants, Marmaduke Ramsay. Even this second attempted visit was not to be. The ship was stopped from landing because of reports of a cholera outbreak in England from where the *Beagle* had just departed. Within a few weeks the *Beagle* reached Santiago in the Cape Verde Islands. They arrived on 16 January and stayed until early February. Being his first landfall, Darwin waxed poetic about the pleasure he felt walking under the tropical sun on a desert island. He found the geology to be the most

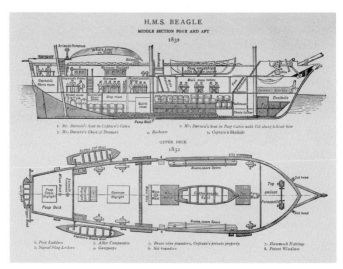

HMS *Beagle*, 1832. At the upper left is Darwin seated in the poop cabin with a hammock slung behind him.

44

interesting aspect of the islands and noted the interplay between volcanic and marine rocks. It allowed him to think geologically, using his nascent training from Sedgwick and testing Lyell's ideas on changing sea levels. He did not ignore the biota, however, and he took special delight in the rapidity of movement and shifting colours of octopuses he found in the tidal pools.

By the end of February 1832 Darwin made his first visit to another continent when the *Beagle* landed at Salvador, Brazil. Primed by Humboldt's accounts of tropical rainforests, Darwin was overwhelmed and delighted by what he saw. He was not so inclined when he witnessed the brutality of slavery in and around the city. By mid-March HMS *Beagle* was heading south, reaching Rio de Janeiro in early April. Letters he received included devastating news from and about his first infatuation, if not first love, Fanny Owen. One letter was from Fanny and another from his sister Emily Catherine.[4] The letters indicated that only ten days after Darwin's departure Fanny had become engaged to another man, whom she married after a few months. Although not engaged, Charles and Fanny had certainly exchanged more than mere pleasantries in their correspondence and outings before the voyage. Darwin salved his wounded feelings and pride in letters he wrote to his sisters, who remained ever supportive.

Of great help to Darwin's spirits was undertaking an inland collecting excursion in the company of Englishman Patrick Lennon, visiting his large estancia or ranch some 160 kilometres (100 mi.) from Rio de Janeiro. This was during much of April and May 1832 while the *Beagle* headed back north to Salvador to check previous soundings. Once again, while on this trek Darwin witnessed and noted the cruelties of slavery, including on the estancia of Lennon who had hosted and helped guide his journey. Upon their return to the *Beagle*, Darwin and FitzRoy had one of their more vociferous arguments over the subject of slavery, this time concerning the slaves at the estancia. Darwin's upbringing compelled him to argue for the equality if not equal status of all humans, or at least of men. While not endorsing slavery per se, FitzRoy's decidedly aristocratic background made him much more paternalistic in his view of how lowly servants should be treated.

FitzRoy noted that when the owner of the estancia asked the slaves if they wished for their freedom, they replied no. Darwin unwisely challenged this assertion by asking FitzRoy if he thought the slaves would answer such a question honestly in the presence of their master. This unleashed FitzRoy's violent temper and as he stormed out he said that he doubted they could continue to share a table. Darwin thought this might be the end of his time on the *Beagle*, but by nightfall all had cooled and FitzRoy apologized, saying that they should continue to share space and a table.[5] They never argued about the subject of slavery again, but this was not the end of FitzRoy's violent rages over the next years of the voyage, nor his bouts of melancholia.

In that same summer of 1832 Darwin wrote to Henslow noting his disdain for the coldness that the Tory politicians showed towards the victims and survivors of slavery, and their inaction in abolishing this continued stain on the nation's moral character. Although he spoke well of the officers on the *Beagle*, one wonders if the Tory that Darwin had in mind was Captain FitzRoy himself.[6] Over the next year news on this topic reoccurred in letters sent and received by Darwin. In June 1833 Darwin wrote in a letter to a Cambridge school chum and life-long correspondent, John M. Herbert, about the 'monstrous stain on our boasted liberty, colonial slavery'.[7] In a letter sent by his sister Susan Elizabeth in October 1833, but certainly not received until many months hence, she wrote that Charles would 'rejoice as much as we do over slavery being abolished' in the colonies. She expressed her grudge at the government's promise to pay the slave-owning planters £20 million for the loss of their free labour but opined that slavery might not have ended in the colonies without this incentive.[8]

As the voyage continued, extended land excursions would become paramount to the voyage for Darwin, both scientifically and because it was the only time he was not sea-sick. An estimate of the time he spent on land is as high as three years and three months with only eighteen months at sea. More recent calculations suggest that he spent about one-third of the voyage exploring on shore, allowing fully two-thirds to battle sea-sickness. In June and July 1832, after retrieving Darwin from his excursion to the estancia, the *Beagle* headed southwards towards Buenos Aires, surveying along the way, later sailing even further south. Several stops south of Buenos Aires would prove pivotal for Darwin in answering his questions about the origins and fates of species in far-flung parts of the globe, and why once-living giant mammals in South America had become extinct. Most importantly, in September 1832 the *Beagle* arrived at the small settlement of Bahía Blanca, a new port about halfway down the eastern coast of Argentina.

Darwin made several coastal forays early in the month and on into November, as well as a second visit in 1833, when he recognized two collecting areas to the east of Bahía Blanca, the nearer being Punta Alta and then Monte Hermosa further east. At Punta Alta, with the help of Syms Covington, a *Beagle* cabin boy who became the official field assistant to Darwin in 1833, they collected fossils of shells and mammals, which thrilled Darwin. Particularly interesting were bones of a giant mammal. A similar specimen – also from Argentinian territory, but to the north – had been assembled by Juan Bautista Bru in Madrid in 1795. Darwin's specimen would prove to be the remains of the same genus of giant ground sloth, *Megatherium*. They also recovered large polygonal bony plates that Darwin related to the much smaller living armadillos of the Americas. Given the fragmentary nature of the finds and their newness to science, it was understandable that Darwin could not fully comprehend what he had found. Many but not all of his questions would be answered when he turned over the material

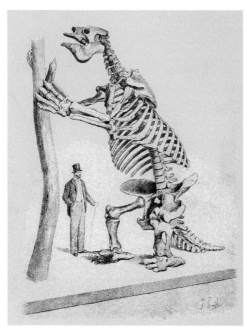

The extinct *Megatherium*, the mammal Darwin found parts of at Bahía Blanca.

to experts in London. This was just the beginning of his journeys in fossil discovery and the questions about these animals would alternatively enthral and vex him for the remainder of the trip.

In December 1832 the *Beagle* continued its surveying much further south, reaching Tierra del Fuego at the southern tip of South America. In addition to their soundings, they had a colonizing mission to perform. On the first voyage of the *Beagle*, during a visit to Tierra del Fuego in December 1828, FitzRoy had assumed command and forcibly taken four native Fuegians whom he planned to return to England for civilizing and Christianizing. We know the original names of three of them, but FitzRoy gave them all Christian names as well. The girl Yokcushlu became Fuegia Basket, the teenage boy Orundellico became Jemmy Button, and the young man Elleparu became York Minster, while the original name of the young man FitzRoy named Boat Memory was not recorded.

FitzRoy had them vaccinated against smallpox in Montevideo, Uruguay, with little effect. Although they were revaccinated once they reached England, Boat Memory contracted smallpox and died in November 1830.

Now FitzRoy was to return to Tierra del Fuego the remaining three in their elevated state along with the missionary Richard Matthews in order to bring English civilization and Christianity to the other natives. The still naive Darwin admitted to the shock of seeing the unkempt local natives covered only in animal skins. He regarded them as the most abject and miserable creatures he had heretofore seen, especially compared to their more educated compatriots dressed in English finery. The small missionary enclave was established at Woolya Cove on the northeast side of Ponsonby Sound with the help of the *Beagle* crew. Darwin held out little hope of success in this remote place. His fears were well founded. Upon the return of the *Beagle* fifteen days later to check on the progress of the enclave they found the encampment in tatters with all supplies either stolen or destroyed along with the primitive structures. A visibly shaken Matthews had been attacked

HMS *Beagle* in the Straits of Magellan, with Mount Sarmiento in the distance.

and molested by the local inhabitants. He chose to come aboard the *Beagle*, where he stayed for the next two years until it reached New Zealand, joining his missionary brother there. The *Beagle* crew did not again see Fuegia Basket or York Minster but over the years after returning to England various reports of the two reached them from other vessels that had visited the region. They would, however, have one more melancholic encounter with Jemmy Button, but this lay some months ahead in their seemingly endless voyage.

After the failed attempt to establish a Christian colony among the Fuegians, the *Beagle* headed in a northeasterly direction, resuming its hydrographic mission upon reaching the Falkland Islands some 485 kilometres (300 mi.) east of the South American coast on 1 March 1833. While the *Beagle* made soundings around the two main and many smaller islands, Darwin explored these bleak outposts of British colonization for which control was re-established that year primarily to hoist the Union Jack and to raise sheep. We can see in his notebooks from this visit, as well as a second visit made at the same time of year in 1834, that Darwin questioned how plants and animals on such islands can resemble similar forms on the mainland yet be clearly marked by differences in the island forms.

What fascinated Darwin most from his second visit in 1834 was what was variously called the Antarctic or Falklands wolf or fox (now *Dusicyon australis*). This canid appeared to be a cross between a wolf and fox in appearance, but decidedly more fox-like in its habits. The locals convinced Darwin that the species occurred, with some variations, only on the islands of East and West Falkland. Darwin could not determine how it had originally reached the islands. He was convinced that it had arrived of its own volition before humans came because it was different from the wild mainland species, but how had it accomplished this seemingly insurmountable task? Evolution was certainly not on Darwin's mind at this point, but nevertheless this case was an early example

The Antarctic or Falklands wolf or fox (*Canis antarcticus*, now *Dusicyon australis*).

which demonstrated to him that a living species on the mainland had reached distant islands. The island species was clearly distinct from the species on the mainland, and these distinctions had probably arisen on the islands. He recalled this example many months later when he once again saw species unique to the Galápagos Islands, but this time it would be many such species, not just one.

Of more immediate concern was the fate of this canid that he correctly predicted would soon vanish from the face of the earth, which it did in 1876, the first canid species to become extinct in historical times. Also, while on the Falklands, Darwin recovered fossils mostly of brachiopods, or 'lamp shells', so-called because of the resemblance of one of the two halves of the shell to an ancient Greek oil lamp. Today some brachiopod species still exist but their heyday was in the Palaeozoic Era, which ended over 250 million years ago. Although brachiopods are very commonly found fossils today, at this time they were little known outside Europe and these forms represented some of the then earliest-known life forms, making their discovery consequential.

In March 1833 FitzRoy made the momentous decision to purchase a second vessel with his own funds to aid what to his mind would be a better hydrographic survey. This would later prove an ill-advised decision because it was done without prior permission of the Admiralty. He placed his first officer, John Clements Wickham, in command of the newly christened HMS *Adventure*, named after the ship of the same name used on the first voyage. The two vessels set a course back to the South American coast, finally arriving in early April 1833 and spending the austral winter in the environs of Maldonado by way of Montevideo, Uruguay. Darwin found accommodations on shore, sometimes quite uncomfortable ones, which allowed him to observe the local people and customs, notably of the quite boisterous gauchos. He geologized in the alpine areas and made considerable zoological collections.

Darwin rejoined the ship, which again sailed south, arriving at the small village of Patagones at the mouth of the Rio Negro in early August 1833. From here Darwin set out northward on what proved to be a six-week inland trek of over 800 kilometres (500 mi.) through the Pampas; he planned to stop briefly to rendezvous with the *Beagle* near Bahía Blanca, where the year before he had discovered fossil mammals. After this meeting Darwin would then head north to Buenos Aires, a journey made especially perilous by civil unrest in the region.

In mid-August 1833 Darwin's small band arrived at Bahía Blanca before the planned rendezvous with the *Beagle*. This afforded him the opportunity to revisit Punta Alta to collect more of the fossils of *Megatherium* that he had earlier recovered. At the nearby Monte Hermosa he found remains of what he thought were fossil rodents and wondered if they might be related to modern forms, although only recently have we learned they probably belong to a completely extinct, solely South American group of mammals. Uncharacteristically Darwin was delighted to board the *Beagle* when it arrived on 27 August at Bahía Blanca. He was able to regale all aboard ship with his adventures among the natives and his first of several encounters with gauchos. He told of their proud and dissolute countenance, their height and their usual attire in ponchos. Knives were always stuck in their belts, which they were quick to use in heated arguments. They were self-sufficient and very skilled in hunting with their bolas. Darwin had tried his hand at throwing these three balls each tethered together by a separate rope. He impressed the gauchos with his horsemanship but made them laugh when during one of his first attempts at throwing the bola it ended up around the legs of his horse. Darwin truly revelled in the free spirit of the gauchos. After this warm reunion at Bahía Blanca in late August, Darwin and his band once again struck out to the north by land towards Buenos Aires on the longest part of the journey.

In order to make the trek, for both permission and safety, Darwin needed to meet and seek the assistance of the commander and later dictator of Argentina, General Juan Manuel de Rosas, who was in the process of eradicating all hostile native peoples from the Pampas. Darwin set out with James Harris, an English trader, and a coterie of rough and tumble gauchos. He met with and gained permission for the journey from Rosas and was permitted to stay at the *postas* or outposts along the way accompanied in part by some of Rosas's men.

This proved to be one of his most memorable inland excursions. On this trip Darwin observed and made notes on many of the plants and animals, including those he collected. He was particularly impressed with native South American forms such as the burrowing rodent known as the tuco-tuco; the guanaco, a camelid; and the native 'ostrich' the rhea. He also noted the gravel plains that he felt supported Charles Lyell's ideas on how such places had once been under the sea, but through gradual processes had been lifted clear of the surface.

Arriving in Buenos Aires on 20 September 1833, Darwin soon decided to head further north along the drainage of the Rio de la Plata. He journeyed towards the town of Santa Fe in the search for more fossils. This proved to be both a rewarding and a puzzling excursion: rewarding because he did find more fossil mammals, but puzzling because among the fossils he recovered were the remains of a mastodon and a horse. Obviously, humans had not brought the mastodon to South America, but what of the horse? Were these the remains of an animal brought by the Spanish or Portuguese, or did it pre-date European colonization? Based on both the geological setting and information he could glean from books in the *Beagle* library he felt it pre-dated European arrival. A number of years in the future, his suspicions would be verified when the horse fossils were identified by the anatomist Richard Owen as pre-European.

When Darwin returned by boat to Buenos Aires to once again join the *Beagle*, he found the city embroiled in revolution. Only by mentioning General Rosas was he able to gain access to the city under a military escort, but he found that when he finally rejoined the *Beagle* they were to remain docked for some time as the crew needed to complete their maps and charts before venturing further. What else could he do but embark on another inland excursion, this time hundreds of kilometres through southern Uruguay. The most remarkable find, or rather acquisition, on this trip was a complete skull of an unknown kind of mammal the size of a small rhinoceros that Darwin purchased from the excavation site's landowner for one shilling and sixpence, about £7 today, still a tremendous bargain for a large fossil mammal skull. He did not know to what the mammal was related and neither did Owen, who would name it *Toxodon* some years later. Only later in the nineteenth century did it become clear that it belonged to a

Darwin's lesser rhea (*Rhea pennata*), top; greater rhea (*Rhea americana*), bottom.

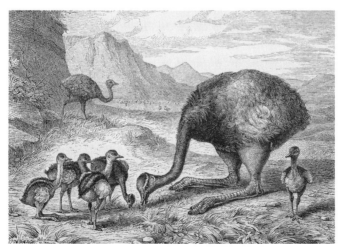

completely extinct group of mammals now called meridungulates, found only in South America, which were as species rich as hoofed mammals in Africa today. According to twenty-first-century molecular work they are thought to be very distant relatives of living tapirs, rhinos and horses.

In early December 1833 the ships set sail south, once again bound for Tierra del Fuego. Near Port Desire the new shipboard artist Conrad Martens, who had replaced the ailing Augustus Earl, shot what all thought was a smaller juvenile common rhea. Earlier, Darwin had heard reports of a smaller rhea species known by the locals as Avestruz Petise occurring to the south of where he had seen the larger form on the Pampas during his inland excursions. After much of the meat was consumed, to his chagrin, Darwin realized their dinner consisted of this smaller species. He was able to salvage much of the head, skin and feathers, which he regarded as a tolerable specimen even if much had been consumed. This smaller form was later named after him. It intrigued him as to how and why living species such as these two forms of rhea distributed themselves separately across the landscape, similarly as to why one found different but related species on the mainland and islands. If created by God, why not the same species in different regions? Thoughts of the changes in species in time and space were probably creeping into his thoughts.

Still further to the south in January 1834 the ships tried to secure fresh water along the coast at Port St Julian. Although the attempt at securing fresh water was abortive, Darwin made his last great fossil mammal find there. It consisted of vertebrae, parts of the pelvis, and limb bones. He thought it another *Mastodon* specimen, but Owen's later work identified it, in part because of its elongate vertebrae, as a relative of llamas, naming it *Macrauchenia*. It had a long neck like a llama or a camel, but we now know it was neither. Along with *Toxodon*, it belongs in same group of completely extinct South American mammals known as meridungulates.

The *Beagle* made a stop in Tierra del Fuego to check on the missionary settlement they had attempted to establish only to find it in total ruins and completely abandoned. While in the region Jemmy Button, now in native garb, approached the *Beagle* in a canoe with his wife, who would not leave the canoe. All exchanged gifts, with FitzRoy receiving otter skins and Darwin some spearheads from Jemmy. FitzRoy could not persuade Jemmy to rejoin them, especially given the entreaties of his wife, still in the canoe. The expedition then headed northeast for one more foray out to the Falkland Islands in March and April 1834 to attempt to satisfy FitzRoy's need for perfection in his charting work. The ships then headed back northwesterly to the mouth of the Río Santa Cruz. Owing to the extreme tides they encountered there, it was possible for them to beach the *Beagle* and check for any damage to her hull they thought might have occurred near Port Desire, but fortunately the damage discovered was easily reparable. Darwin accompanied FitzRoy and a few others on an expedition up Río Santa Cruz in three whale boats. Because of the swift current it proved an arduous journey, which they abandoned within sight of the Andes.

HMS *Beagle* laid ashore for repairs, Río Santa Cruz, Patagonia, 1834.

Although the work was gruelling, Darwin made observations of the geological exposures, which, following the lead of Lyell, Darwin indicated were sediments that had been laid down on the bottom of the sea and gradually lifted up at a later time.

From May into June 1834 the *Beagle* and the *Adventure* traversed and surveyed the channels through Tierra del Fuego before finally reaching the Pacific Ocean on 11 June. There they began to survey the Chilean coastal regions and larger islands such as Chiloe over the next fifteen months. When the *Beagle* arrived in Valparaíso on 23 July, letters awaited Darwin, including praise from Henslow for all the wonderful specimens he had sent back to England.[9] In August and September 1834 Darwin took his first of three journeys into the Andes. This six-week trip on horseback travelled first north into the mountains and then followed a clockwise direction east, south and west back to the coast at Navidad. Near Valparaíso the observation of shell beds above the waterline was added proof that similar areas had been gradually lifted from the sea.

When Darwin returned to the *Beagle* in October 1834, he found that FitzRoy had suffered a mental breakdown and relinquished his command to Wickham. The incident was precipitated by FitzRoy's receipt of a letter from the Admiralty that not only disapproved of his purchase of the *Adventure* but ordered him to sell it, fortunately at a small profit. After considerable cajoling, FitzRoy was persuaded to resume command. With FitzRoy again in command the *Beagle* resumed its charting and map surveying of the Chilean coast. Upon reaching Valdivia in late February 1835, the crew experienced what some called the worst earthquake ever to hit the region. It destroyed most of the town and when they reached Concepción to the north they found the destruction there to be widespread. Ever the geologist, Darwin was impressed that the earthquake had raised the coast by a number of metres; it was again proof of Lyell's up-and-down movement of land relative to seas, though a somewhat more rapid example in this case.

Darwin's second and most adventuresome Andean trek – this time riding mules over the 5,800-metre (19,000 ft) Portillo Pass – began on 18 March 1835 from Santiago. On this excursion he found marine fossils in the high Andes and was enthralled that this discovery meant the mountains had been lifted thousands of metres above sea level. The group descended the Andes east towards Mendoza, Argentina. While exploring the Argentinian side of the mountain range Darwin was bitten by a vinchuca or kissing bug; he became quite ill, probably with Chagas disease, now known to be a vector for a trypanosome, a parasitic protozoan. This is one of the maladies that has been thought to have plagued Darwin throughout his life once he returned to England. On the return journey the group crossed back over the Andes through the Uspallata Range, finally arriving back at the Chilean coast on 10 April. On 24 April 1835 Darwin made his third and final Andean trek, collecting as he went, this time along the western flank north and inland from Valparaíso, arriving back at the coast at Coquimbo on 5 July.

The *Beagle*, with Darwin once more aboard, headed north, arriving on 19 July at Callao Bay, Lima, Peru. After reprovisioning for the long sail west across the vast Pacific Ocean, the ship departed on 7 September bound for the equatorially perched Galápagos archipelago, which was sighted eight days later. These volcanically formed islands, 965 kilometres (600 mi.) west of Ecuador, are true isolated oceanic islands, meaning they never had a land connection with South America. Based on the accounts of previous visitors, Darwin hoped to see erupting volcanos, but he saw only fumaroles, vents emitting volcanic gases. He did witness vast areas of lava-strewn desolation, a cacophony of large lizards, the most northerly penguins, and giant land tortoises. From Lima he wrote to his sister Caroline that although he greatly anticipated the zoology and geology of the Galápagos, he was equally anxious to once again sight England's shores. He was not alone in this

Different varieties of Galápagos tortoises.

longing for home as all aboard were growing weary of the voyage that had now stretched to more than three and a half years.[10]

The name 'Galápagos' is shrouded in conflicting legends. Similar words from quite ancient Spanish refer to the carapace or shell of turtles, or in this case the tortoises of these islands. The name is also said to derive from the upturned carapace of some of these tortoises and its resemblance to the shape of a certain kind of Spanish saddle. To add intrigue to the naming game, they have also been known as the Islas Encantadas, or Enchanted Isles. This was a somewhat ironic name because the enchantment of the islands derives from the fog that can cloak them as well as the frequently treacherous currents between them. Whatever the true source or sources of these names, the islands both delighted and puzzled Darwin no end and were to play an important role in the nascent development of his ideas on evolution that were to emerge a few years later, if not while on the voyage itself.

The *Beagle* remained in the Galápagos environs for only four and a half weeks. Darwin went ashore for the first time on 17 September 1835 at Chatham Island (now San Cristóbal). Between then and 17 October, Darwin and his companions visited four islands, including Charles (Floreana), Albermarle (Isabela) and James (Santiago) islands, spending parts of nineteen days onshore, with the longest stretch at ten days on James Island. He even hoped to find fossils on the Galápagos, yet this was unlikely because of the islands' mostly volcanic composition, which tended to destroy rather than preserve fossils. Here he was disappointed, yet a crew member brought him a fossil shell from a large exposure of volcanic sandstone on a small island off Charles Island – the only mention of a fossil while in the Galápagos.

If the geology intrigued Darwin, the animals astounded him. Their naivety was a delightful surprise. He made sizeable collections of both plants and animals from the land and sea. Very uncharacteristically for him, Darwin failed to carefully note from which islands some specimens came. This was especially true of the small brownish birds with beaks of varying sizes that did not seem to differ much from island to island. Although he did not appear to detect a relationship between these small, rather nondescript birds, he was able to differentiate at least three or more species. Upon returning to England he was chagrined to learn that these little birds represented upwards of thirteen different interrelated species that we now call Darwin's or Galápagos finches, even though molecular work has now shown them to be tanagers. His reputation was spared as a careful keeper of field notes because other crew members, including FitzRoy, had made careful notes as to where specimens of these little birds occurred.

Darwin was not so cavalier in recording locality data for other species – notably tortoises, large lizards and mockingbirds. He recorded in his notes that the Ecuadorean governor of the islands, the Englishman Nicholas O. Lawson, claimed he could identify

1. Geospiza magnirostris.
2. Geospiza fortis.
3. Geospiza parvula.
4. Certhidea olivacea.

Four species of Galápagos finches (now tanagers).

from which island any tortoise or its shell came. This once again emphasized the uniqueness of animals to each island. Darwin noted the fate of many tortoises at the hand of man. In the past, a single vessel may have taken away seven hundred individuals and a frigate was reported as taking two hundred in one day. Darwin had some concern as to whether the tortoises were native or had been brought to the islands. Upon returning to England he was informed that they were indeed Galápagos natives. Today the tortoises are usually placed in one species, *Chelonoidis nigra*, with populations varying on the different islands, just as Darwin recorded, with their shell morphologies often related to the habitats in which they live and feed. On dry, lowland areas of the islands, the tortoises are smaller, with saddleback-shaped shells that permit the animals to reach tall plants with their long necks. In the more humid highlands of other islands, the tortoises tend to be larger, with domed shells and shorter necks for grazing lower to the ground.

Of the species of iguana, Darwin paid most attention to two: what he thought was a single species of marine iguana that he found particularly hideous, and what he thought was one species of large land iguana. Upon dissection, Darwin found that both were herbivorous. The land form had a variety of plant material in its gut; the marine form had only seaweed, leading him to correctly surmise that its physical attributes of stubby nose, clawed feet and flattened tail showed it was the only truly marine lizard in the world.

Among birds, Darwin was especially enamoured with mockingbirds, which seemed to vary more visibly than did the finches. He noted as many as four distinct varieties or species through the various islands. Most importantly Darwin discerned the resemblances of many of the Galápagos species to similar ones across South America. We see in the Galápagos just the faintest glimmer of what Darwin would later contemplate regarding the non-fixity of species – the ability of species to change over time.

The Galápagos served as the jumping-off place for the nearly year-long, mostly oceanic journey home, with ample time for contemplation, even for a sea-sick naturalist. In hindsight we know the importance the islands eventually played in evolutionary theorizing by Darwin, namely that the ancestors of life forms on these islands came from South America and once in the Galápagos evolved into their present forms on the various islands. On 20 October the *Beagle* departed the Galápagos for the 5,150-kilometre (3,200 mi.) sail to Tahiti, which it reached on 15 November 1835. After a ten-day stay it departed again, reaching New Zealand on 21 December. The *Beagle* then sailed on to Australia, arriving in early 1836 with three stops in Sydney, Hobart and the southwestern coast. On his inland excursions he was able to see marsupials such as kangaroos and even the unusual egg-laying platypus – the true relationships of both among mammals elsewhere in the world were still in considerable doubt. Later, in his 1839 book on the voyage, he mused about these encounters, carefully couching his words as a quote. 'An unbeliever in every thing beyond his own reason might exclaim, "Two distinct Creators must have been at work; their object, however, has been the same, and certainly the end in each case is complete."'[11] His readers would not have known but by 1839 when he wrote this oblique reference to evolution he had already been writing in his private notebooks for about two years concerning this very topic.

While traversing the Indian Ocean in April 1836 the *Beagle* visited the Cocos and then Mauritius islands. Throughout the voyage Darwin had noted the growth and formation of corals and the reefs that they built, but this came even more into focus for him in Tahiti, the Cocos and Mauritius. He noted as others before him that coral reefs frequently form a partial or complete encirclement of lagoons. Some ten years later he was able to present his findings in a book about how these atolls grew upwards as their central mountains eroded away.

At the end of May 1836 the *Beagle* arrived in Cape Town in southern Africa. The two most momentous events here for Darwin were his meetings with two men, one of whom was the Scottish physician and naturalist Andrew Smith. Some ten years earlier Smith had been nominated as the first Superintendent of the South African Museum of Natural History in Cape Town. Smith greatly influenced Darwin's ideas about what kind of environment was required for large herbivorous quadrupeds such as elephants. On the South American Pampas Darwin found few large native herbivorous quadrupeds. He concluded that the lack of luxuriant vegetation was the cause of this absence, and further that the giant ground sloths, giant armadillo relatives and mastodons had all succumbed because climate change had caused the loss of vegetation needed to sustain these great beasts. Smith disabused him of this notion: they rode some distance together into the scantily vegetated southern African plains, where Smith told Darwin of the great number of large herbivorous quadrupeds, such as elephants, rhinoceros, hippopotamuses, giraffe, wildebeest and various antelope species sustained by this environment. Darwin was able to see enough of this herbivore diversity to convince him of the veracity of Smith's arguments. He would need other reasons, therefore, to account for the loss of the large herbivores on the Pampas. The two maintained an infrequent correspondence over the years.

The second meeting in Cape Town, accompanied by Captain FitzRoy, was with the renowned English astronomer John Herschel, who had arrived with his wife in southern Africa in January 1834. He was there to study the heavens of the southern hemisphere. Herschel had read and greatly appreciated the geological writings of Charles Lyell and what his ideas might portend regarding the appearances of new species after the extinction of older ones. In a letter to Lyell, the contents of which became public, Herschel referred to this appearance of new species as 'that mystery of mysteries'.[12] Years later Herschel's opinions influenced Darwin's ideas as he developed his theories of evolution. Darwin took Herschel's dictum to heart, even citing the above quote in his magnum opus on evolution that was published 25 years later. Ironically, Herschel rejected the mechanism of natural selection that Darwin was to later propose to explain evolution. In a final quirk of fate, Herschel and Darwin were buried in adjoining floor crypts in Westminster Abbey: Herschel in 1871 and Darwin in 1882.

In mid-June the *Beagle* departed Cape Town, with stops at St Helena and Ascension islands, but instead of heading straight for England, to the consternation of the crew, FitzRoy insisted that they take a detour back across the Atlantic Ocean to recheck soundings off eastern Brazil. With this accomplished they then headed to England with a stop at the Azores. On 2 October 1836 HMS *Beagle* anchored at Falmouth after a voyage of four years and nine months. Darwin made a hasty departure for Shrewsbury and his home, The Mount, where his family awaited his return.

What of the fate of HMS *Beagle*, a vessel that was to become one of the most famous surveying ships in Royal Navy history as a result of Darwin's voyage? One more survey expedition awaited her. Six months later, after repairs, she set sail to survey the coast of Australia. Between 1837 and 1843, the *Beagle* was under the command of John Clements Wickham, who had been second in command under FitzRoy, and Charles's former cabin mate, John Lort Stokes, was the first officer. They honoured their former shipmates FitzRoy and Darwin in naming a river in the northern reaches of what would become Western Australia after the former captain and a port in what is now Northern Territory after the young naturalist. As is the case for many similar ships, her fate after the third voyage was inglorious; she ended her existence as a permanently anchored coastguard watch vessel in the Thames Estuary.

4

A New Scientific Career and a New Wife

After an almost two-day journey from Falmouth, where the *Beagle* docked for the evening of 2 October 1836, Darwin arrived at his family home in Shrewsbury early on the morning of 4 October. In addition to his family finding him considerably underweight, they thought the shape of his head visibly altered after the long voyage (possibly in jest, calling upon the tired trope of phrenology). Apart from the just completed five years on the *Beagle*, the next ten years would prove among the headiest in Darwin's life. It would certainly prove to be one of the most stimulating and busiest intervals. His first task required the unloading of the many crates of material he had sent back to England in the care of John Henslow. It was then necessary for him to seek out able scientists ready, willing and capable of evaluating and describing his hard-won specimens. His oversight was required in the publication of these specimens, and he needed to provide introductions to the volumes that would result from their description. FitzRoy asked Darwin to contribute a volume of his experiences and a natural history of the voyage as part of a multi-volume work. Separately, Darwin would also prepare three additional, somewhat technical, books on the various aspects of the geological surveys undertaken during the voyage.

In the midst of the preparations of volumes about the voyage and its specimens, Darwin began what at first was a more guarded pursuit. Commencing in the summer of 1837, less than a year after his return, he opened notebooks dealing with his ruminations on John Herschel's 'mystery of mysteries', how new species appear. Over the course of three years Darwin was to pen nine notebooks – or at least those are what have been preserved. Of these, five dealt with his emerging ideas on the origin of new species. In part based on his labelling, we call these the Red Notebook and Notebooks B, C, D and E. Although probably not intentionally kept secret, they were nonetheless useful for his private musings at the time on how new species might appear. As we unequivocally see in these notebooks, by July 1837 Darwin had become more confident of the validity of evolution. In Notebook B, started at this time, we have his now famous branching diagram that he labelled 'I think.'[1] Notebook B is proof positive that by the summer of 1837 Darwin was moving ahead in his theorizing about evolution, but there is evidence that he began to contemplate its possibility on his homeward journey aboard the *Beagle*. A sad coda is that Notebook B, along with Notebook C, went missing from the Cambridge University Library in 2001, not being reported until late 2020 and now presumed stolen. Fortunately, very good copies exist.

Determining how much earlier Darwin began to realize that evolution occurs before he penned Notebook B remains a contentious issue. Darwin never wrote that he began developing his ideas on evolution while on the *Beagle*, but some of his surviving comments written sometime after leaving the Galápagos but before reaching England suggest that he was indeed contemplating evolution at that time. He had noted that the unusual distributions of animals on the Galápagos and Falkland Islands led him to doubt the permanence of species. His *Ornithological Notes*, published in 1963 and edited by his granddaughter Nora Barlow, included a transcribed version of the comments that Darwin wrote concerning bird observations and collections he had made while on the *Beagle* as she headed north from southern Africa back to England. In these

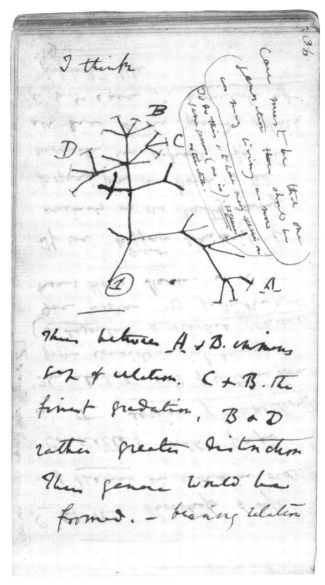

Darwin's first phylogeny or tree of life, his famous 1837 'I think' diagram from Notebook B.

notes he recollected that Spaniards could say from which of the Galápagos Islands a tortoise derived based on body form, shape of scales and general size. He wrote that these scantily stocked islands often in sight of each other are occupied by birds that vary little from island to island yet fill the same roles in nature, suggesting that they are only varieties derived from a common South American ancestor. He went on to note similar small differences between the Falkland Islands fox of the east and west islands. He concluded, 'If there is the slightest foundation for these remarks, the Zoology of Archipelagos will be well worth examining; for such facts would undermine the stability of species.'[2] Opinions vary on what this last sentence means. The most straightforward answer is that shortly before Darwin reached England, he had grappled with the question about the immutability of species and had decided that species in fact do change over time.

In his *Autobiography*, first published in 1887, five years after his death, Darwin had written that soon after his return from the voyage he began querying breeders and gardeners about methods for their selection of traits they desired to preserve. In October 1838, Darwin read *An Essay on the Principle of Population* (1798) by Thomas Malthus. This was a treatise theorizing that the unsustainability of unchecked human population growth would lead to famine and death, ultimately decreasing the population size. Darwin argued that the struggle for existence also occurred in the animal and plant realms, meaning that those with favourable traits would survive whereas those with unfavourable traits would perish. As these favourable traits accumulated, new species would form and over generations would become better adapted to their environment. In his Notebook D he wrote that with this realization he now had the mechanism for evolution, what he would come to call 'natural selection'.

The tasks at hand when Darwin arrived back in England began in earnest just a few weeks after his return. He visited Henslow in Cambridge to discuss the receival, storage and distribution of the myriad specimens he had collected on the voyage. Syms Covington, who had assisted Darwin on the *Beagle* and on a number of his collecting excursions, agreed to remain with Darwin as his amanuensis and manservant, at least until the unpacking and sorting of specimens could be completed. Covington planned to then emigrate to Australia, which he did, arriving in 1840, but in the meantime the organizing of the collections would at times prove a difficult and thankless task.

Soon Darwin was in London visiting all the major scientific institutions in his attempts to drum up interest among various scientists for his collections. There was interest among geologists, but many zoologists baulked at the laboriously trying task of describing new species, of which Darwin had many. This was a time when many exotic new specimens were arriving from a host of global expeditions from all around Britain's vast empire. It did help that Darwin's reputation preceded him.

In November 1835, while Darwin was still on the *Beagle*, Henslow had distributed some of Darwin's correspondence in a private publication to the Cambridge Philosophical Society. That same month his former Cambridge professor and able geological field tutor Adam Sedgwick presented some of Darwin's South American work to the Geological Society of London. This meant that Darwin was already a budding scientific celebrity even before he had again set foot in England in early October 1836. Within months of his return Darwin became a member of the Geological Society of London and presented his first three papers, which dealt with geology and palaeontology, in January 1837. Shortly thereafter he was appointed a member of the society's council. An added bonus was that his father, Robert, now realized that Charles would never become a country parson, but rather had a bright future as a gentleman naturalist. With this in mind Charles received a handsome annual allowance of £400 as well as stock investments from his father, setting him up to pursue science full time.

In December 1836 Darwin settled into rooms on Fitzwilliam Street in Cambridge to begin work on his collection. While there he dined regularly at Christ's College, where he had received his undergraduate degree in 1831. He noted that he was not able to recognize any of the undergraduates – it was not uncommon for a recipient of a bachelor of arts degree at Cambridge to receive a master of arts two years after receiving their bachelor's degree. The now increasingly well-known Darwin received his master's degree in December 1836. His financial records showed that his three years while an undergraduate had cost slightly over £636 and that he had paid £14 for his undergraduate degree and £12 for his postgraduate degree. Cambridge did not charge him for the honorary doctorate (LL.D.) that was to be bestowed upon him in 1877. In all of the many books yet to flow from his mind and pen, he would list various honours and affiliations after his name on the title page. Always first was his MA and then his LL.D., of which he was rightfully very proud.

By early 1837 Darwin realized that he needed to be in London, closer to the scientific experts and institutions essential for his work, notably those whom he would enlist in the descriptions of his specimens. Thus, in March, he moved to rooms at 36 Great Marlborough Street. Once there he often visited one of his scientific idols and now friend, geologist Charles Lyell. On one occasion in October 1836 Lyell had introduced Darwin to Richard Owen. This anatomist and palaeontologist was then Hunterian professor at the Royal College of Surgeons. He agreed to describe the fossil mammals collected on the voyage. For the time being the two remained amicable if not close colleagues, but this would sour beyond repair when Owen became an implacable and jealous foe of the evolutionary ideas that Darwin would propose almost a quarter of a century later. Ironically, Owen demonstrated that the fossil

Richard Owen, palaeontological friend, then foe, of Darwin.

mammals Darwin found were more closely related to forms living in present-day South America, strengthening Darwin's argument that living species most often resembled their fossil ancestors from the same region.

Living in London afforded Darwin other opportunities. In 1838 Charles Lyell helped in Darwin's election to the Athenaeum Club because of his renown surrounding the voyage of the HMS

Charles Lyell, famed English geologist and Darwin supporter, late 1860s.

Beagle. This private club was founded in 1824 by men of status and inherited wealth; early on it was especially men of the clergy who were granted membership, but later it opened its doors to men of distinction in the arts, literature and sciences. It did not admit women until 2002. Because he was in London, Darwin frequented the club's excellent library. There he continued to write in his notebooks on his emerging ideas of evolution. In addition to Charles Lyell, the club's members included those who would become some of Darwin's best friends and colleagues.

A notable opportunity for Darwin while living in London was his visit and observations of a young female orangutan at the London Zoo. The three-year-old orangutan named Lady Jane (but known as Jenny) was the first of her species shown at the zoo. She had been purchased from a sailor for £150 in late 1837. The zoo tried to increase her appeal by dressing her in Western attire and teaching her to drink tea. This was the first live great ape Darwin had ever seen and he was intrigued. He had already begun conjecturing in

Jenny, the captive orangutan at London Zoo, in the *Penny Magazine of the Society for the Diffusion of Useful Knowledge*, 3 February 1838.

private about the connection between great apes and the origin of humans. For him this meant that humans were not the pinnacle of creation we had been taught. Over several visits he witnessed a variety of behaviours: her childlike tantrum upon being denied an apple by her keeper, her intrigue on seeing herself in a mirror, and her ability to obey instructions. For Darwin this provided a strong impression of what he was coming to realize as evolutionary connections of humans to other species. The fate of Jenny was not a happy one. She died at about five years of age in 1839, the same year that Darwin's first child was born. Darwin observed and wrote about his son in much the same way as he had with Jenny.

In early January 1837 Darwin presented his bird and mammal specimens to the Zoological Society of London. Darwin visited the ornithologist John Gould, the first curator and preserver in the museum of the society, so that he might identify the bird specimens and possibly agree to describe them. While Darwin had been enamoured with the three or four different kinds of mockingbirds he had identified in the Galápagos, it was the nondescript small brownish-black birds from these islands that proved a profound revelation. His locality data for these small birds had been spotty but he had been saved by the information of his shipmates. Based on these specimens and the reinforced locality data, Gould identified this group of twelve species as finches found only on these islands. He reported his findings to the Zoological Society in January 1837, creating enough of a stir that the newspapers reported on the discovery. In addition to the finches, mockingbirds and other birds from the Galápagos, Gould informed Darwin that the rhea he had salvaged from the stew pot in December 1833 was a smaller new species, which Gould named for him. Darwin and Gould reported about the South American common and small rheas in consecutive talks to the society.[3]

Darwin hoped to present the zoological and palaeontological results of the expedition in a series of well-illustrated large-format publications to be called *The Zoology of the Voyage of HMS Beagle*. This format permitted very large and often coloured plates, and even huge fold-out plates in the case of the fossil mammal volumes. *Zoology* was to appear in five parts as nineteen separate unbound publications called numbers, which for an extra, small cost could be bound in three to five volumes. Darwin had been able to secure £1,000 in public funding for the project and the publisher Smith, Elder & Co. had agreed to do the printing. Darwin planned to include both vertebrates and invertebrates, but this was not to be, especially as the funding proved insufficient, with the publisher and Darwin needing to advance additional funds to complete its publication. Owen had already agreed to describe the fossil mammals and in early 1838 his was to become the first of four numbers on this topic that would appear from 1838 to 1843. This was followed by George Robert Waterhouse's four numbers on mammals (1838–9). The ornithological work was complicated by Gould and his illustrator wife Elizabeth's departure to Australia in 1838. Fortunately, Gould was able to complete the descriptions, which included the very fine illustrations by Elizabeth which graced the five separate publications on birds that composed Part 3 of the *Zoology* (1838–42). Sadly, after returning to England, in 1841 Elizabeth died at the age of only 37 from complications with the birth of her eighth child. Leonard Jenyns's four numbers on fishes (1840–42) and Thomas Bell's two numbers on reptiles and amphibians (1842–3) rounded out the publication.

While all of the contributions in the *Zoology* undoubtedly contributed to the mid-nineteenth-century growth in knowledge of the world's biota, it was the fossil mammal and bird volumes that had the greatest influence on Darwin's private musings on evolution. For Darwin, the extinct giant ground sloths and massive armadillo-like glyptodonts that Owen described were clearly earlier harbingers of the modern living sloths and armadillos found almost exclusively in South America. This demonstrated to Darwin the separate successions of mammals through time on each of the different continents. Similarly, the unique Galápagos finches and mockingbirds described by Gould pointed directly to South America as their ancestral source. Once the ancestral forms reached the Galápagos, they produced new species as they colonized the various islands.

Beyond work on the vertebrates for the voyage, Darwin was able to persuade the entomologist Francis Walker and the naturalist George Waterhouse, who had described the living mammals of the *Beagle* voyage, to publish about 25 articles on insects. The conchologist and illustrator George Sowerby agreed to describe and illustrate fossil shells in appendices to Darwin's two books in 1844 and 1846 which dealt with the geology of South America. Also, the German naturalist Christian Ehrenberg published four papers in German on the group of microscopically sized organisms then collectively lumped together as Infusoria.

Turning then to who might describe the plants that Darwin had collected on the voyage, Darwin saw as a natural choice his mentor John Henslow, who expressed interest and began to catalogue and examine the finds. Henslow sought help with identifications from William Jackson Hooker, then at the University of Glasgow and later director of Kew Gardens, London. Hooker contacted Darwin in 1843 to ask whether his son Joseph Dalton Hooker, eight years Darwin's junior, might be allowed to describe the plants. Hooker had just returned from a voyage to the Antarctic on HMS *Erebus* that had lasted from 1839 to 1843. He had served as assistant to Robert McCormick, the ship's surgeon as well as the person in charge of collecting scientific specimens. This was the same McCormick who left HMS *Beagle* in Rio de Janeiro in April 1832 only a few months into its second voyage because he felt that Captain FitzRoy favoured Darwin in scientific matters. Hooker's voyage on HMS *Erebus* was followed by expeditions of varying lengths to the Indian Himalayas, Palestine, Morocco and the western United States.

Joseph Dalton Hooker, famed English botanist, colleague and good friend of Darwin.

Given his experience, all agreed that the younger Hooker was up to this task, which he was, publishing papers on the Galápagos plants and their distributions in the 1840s. Even more importantly, J. D. Hooker became one of Darwin's closest friends and professional confidantes as Darwin began to fill notebooks on his emerging ideas on evolution. Hooker's critiques, advice and friendship would prove invaluable to Darwin.

In early discussions FitzRoy had asked Darwin if he could provide text to include in his own book that he was preparing on the second voyage of the *Beagle*. Later, with the consent of FitzRoy and the urging of his friends, Darwin prepared his own narrative of the voyage. Darwin completed his manuscript for the multi-volume work in June 1837, well ahead of the other contributions. The four-volume work finally appeared in print in 1839. The first volume was on the first voyage by its commander Philip King, the second volume and an appendix were by Robert FitzRoy on the second voyage, and Darwin's contribution on natural history and terrestrial excursions constituted the third volume. This was his first authored book and he was thrilled on its publication. His contribution bore the simple title *Journal and Remarks*. It was so successful that its publisher Henry Colburn reissued it as a separate volume that same year as *Journal of Researches into the Geology and Natural History of the Various Countries Visited by HMS Beagle*. By most accounts this was Darwin's most successful book, never having been out of print and translated into many languages. Its title has changed at least four times but is now usually known as *The Voyage of the Beagle.* FitzRoy found the great popularity of this volume irksome, and its success bothered him even more as he felt Darwin's treatment of the geology observed in South America lacked any recourse to biblical explanations, which he felt compelled to include in his own contribution to counteract what Darwin had written. In his telling, by taking Darwin on the voyage he had harboured a viper in his bosom.

Darwin's almost five years on the *Beagle* had clearly not satiated his desire for geological fieldwork. In the summer of 1838 he headed north, combining a visit with his family in Shrewsbury with a trip to the Scottish Highlands to have a look at the Parallel Roads of Glen Roy. Local lore identified these strikingly parallel terraces at three different levels as some sort of animal tracks or human roads. In the nineteenth century they caught the eye of geologists.

The Parallel Roads of Glen Roy, Scotland.

Fresh from his sojourn on the *Beagle*, Darwin thought with youthful hubris that he could easily apply what he had learned about South American marine terraces to this Scottish landform. Following the lead of Lyell's thinking Darwin speculated that the rise and fall of the sea level had formed these so-called parallel roads. He presented his findings in a talk and then monograph in 1839, but only a year later the Swiss-born palaeontologist and geologist Louis Agassiz, who developed the idea of ice ages, pronounced these were formed by the freezing and thawing of ice on lakes associated with massive glaciers. Darwin defended his conclusions for over twenty years but eventually Agassiz's idea of ice ages and ice lakes took hold, forcing Darwin to finally concede that his conclusions were a great geological blunder.

His visit to Glen Roy, his papers presented at Society meetings and the preparation of his narrative of the *Beagle* voyage provided a heady scientific life for Darwin. His personal life was soon to take an equally dramatic turn. Ever the scientist, in the spring and summer of 1838 Darwin took time to write lists on the pros and cons of marriage. The best known of these he most likely wrote that summer. On two side-by-side lists, which he headed 'Marry' on one side and on the other 'Not Marry', he wrote out his reasons for each. Under the longer 'Marry' list he wrote themes such as 'children – (if it please God)', 'constant companion', 'friend in old age', 'object to be beloved & played with' and 'better than a dog anyhow', 'charms of music & female chitchat', 'intolerable to think of living life like a neuter bee', and imagine living a solitary life in a 'smoky, dirty London house'. Under the heading 'Not Marry', he listed lack of freedom to go where one liked, expense and anxiety of children, loss of time and less money for books. He decided emphatically at the end of the two lists, when he wrote 'Marry– Mary–Marry Q.E.D.'[4] He did not tarry long; on 11 November 1838 Darwin proposed to his first cousin Emma Wedgwood and she immediately accepted. This was not a surprise within the Darwin and Wedgwood families as the two had known each other all their lives, and Emma was only nine months older than Charles. They married shortly thereafter on 29 January 1839. Only five days before, just shy of his thirtieth birthday, he had been elected one of the youngest Fellows of the Royal Society, the oldest national scientific institution in the world. Both his personal and professional lives were moving forward apace.

As it turned out, it was fortunate for Darwin that his first love Fanny Owen was fickle, forsaking him for another man almost as soon as Darwin had left on the *Beagle* in late 1831. Given the role normally assigned to married women in the early Victorian era one can only marvel at the strengths of Emma in all matters. She was a confidante, friend, lover and mother to the ten children she bore with him. Although Emma was deeply religious and worried for his immortal soul, she could find it in her heart and mind to support Charles throughout their lives as he slowly moved away from any vestiges of religious belief. In turn Charles never ridiculed her beliefs, thus tamping down any obvious differences on religious matters. There was mutual respect. They were very indulgent parents who allowed their children considerable freedom, much as Charles had experienced at The Mount and Emma had at Maer Hall. The only true familial sorrows they faced together were the deaths of three of their children and a young daughter-in-law.

A few months before Charles and Emma were married, Darwin rented a home at 12 Upper Gower Street in London. They christened it Macaw Cottage because of its gaudy colours and furnishings. The first two of their ten children were born there: William Erasmus in late 1839 and Anne 'Annie' Elizabeth in early 1841. Darwin certainly must have had his observations of the young orangutan Jenny in mind when he took a special interest in recording the mental development of his two young children. This was especially true with William, for whom he kept regular records from his birth until he was almost five years old. Darwin did the same with Annie, but with less detail. He and sometimes Emma did so with later children, but not to the extent he had done

George Richmond, portraits of Emma Darwin and Charles Darwin, late 1830s, watercolour.

with William. As with any new parent Darwin was interested in the growth and development of his and Emma's children, but Darwin's curiosity went beyond that of a doting father. As a scientist he had the ability to somewhat detach himself from the role of father into that of more impartial observer, a characteristic which had served him well on the *Beagle* and now would do so as an aspiring young scientist. Darwin noted those characteristics of William that were reflexive and instinctual, such as sneezing, hiccuping, stretching, sucking and screaming, versus those that clearly showed progressive learning about the world around him. Darwin was also interested in the degree to which these developmental features could be found in other, what he called 'lower', animals. These interests would culminate many years later in his 1872 book *The Expression of the Emotions in Man and Animals*. He had not forgotten his observations of William, for a few years later he also published 'A Biographical Sketch of an Infant' in the journal *Mind*. This article was destined to become a classic; it is still read today on university psychology courses.

Not only was Darwin busy in observing the development of his first child, but he was approaching his early work on evolutionary theory. Although at this time his musings on evolution still remained a guarded pursuit, he was now seeking information from others that might help him. In 1839, while still on Upper Gower Street, he had an eight-page questionnaire privately printed by Stewart & Murray of London titled 'Questions about the Breeding of Animals'. There were 21 questions printed on each page in single columns so that the responder had space to add in their answers next to the queries. Exactly how many and to whom the questionnaire was distributed is not known. Two known responses came from neighbours near the Wedgwood estate at Maer Hall. We know from Darwin's notebooks of the time that he was actively contemplating transmutation and natural selection. Although nothing of this appears in this questionnaire, his queries on breeding certainly show what he was thinking about: artificial selection. This was the process that farmers and breeders used in the breeding of plants and animals. For Darwin, his natural selection was much the same process, but instead of humans performing the selection it was controlled by nature. For the rest of his life Darwin continued the practice of sending out many requests for information and specimens from people all over the world.

5

A Momentous Move

As the family began to grow, they wished to escape London's filth and crowding. In 1842 they purchased Down House, about 26 kilometres (16 mi.) southeast of central London on Luxted Road, very near the village of what is now known as Downe, Kent. When the Darwins arrived the village lacked the terminal 'e'. As the story goes, the change to the current name came later in the 1940s, to avoid confusion for the Royal Mail with County Down in Ireland. In addition to the quite young William and Annie, the Darwin family were accompanied by Joseph Parslow, who joined the household on Upper Gower Street as manservant to Darwin soon after Charles and Emma were married. He would remain with the Darwins for 36 years before retiring in 1875. Upon his death in 1898 he was buried in St Mary's the Virgin churchyard, where many members of the Darwin family also lie. His headstone in part reads 'faithful servant and friend of Charles Darwin'. Parslow would come to be more than a manservant to Darwin, however. Over the years at Down House he would assist in Darwin's scientific endeavours, be a companion in billiard games, and serve as nurse and shower man for the 'water cure' treatments Darwin took daily in his home-built facility.

Not all went well during the Darwin family's move. In September 1842, only a matter of days after Charles and Emma had arrived at Down House, their third child Mary Eleanor was born. A mere 23 days later in October their newborn died of unknown causes. Although they mourned her death, additional children came in rather quick succession. Just the next year their fourth child, Henrietta 'Etty', was born, followed by George in 1845. Five more were to be born from 1847 through to 1856 – Elizabeth, Francis, Leonard, Horace and Charles – completing the Darwin brood. Darwin would maintain Down House as his residence until he died in 1882, never again leaving England's shores. Still, this was not to be the life of a parson in a quiet country parish that he briefly contemplated while at the University of Cambridge, but certainly he would follow the other part of that old plan, pursuing his interests in natural history.

It must be emphasized that Down House would become not only the home where the Darwin family lived and the children grew up, but the scientific laboratory for Darwin for the next forty years until his death. The beginnings were not auspicious according to Darwin. In a letter to his sister Emily Catherine from July 1842 he describes Down House in considerable detail, at one point writing that it was 'ugly, [and] looks neither old nor new', so within a year of arriving they began making changes.[1] One issue was that the height of Luxted Road as it passed in front of the house afforded them little privacy. Darwin had the road lowered to provide more seclusion and to improve drainage. A room facing towards the gardens on the southwest would later become the dining room. Its ceiling was raised, and a bay window inserted as well. An extension was planned in 1876 for the northeast side of the house and completed in 1877. The addition was planned as a billard room, but in 1881 Darwin took over occupancy, calling it his 'new study', eschewing the study that he had used since 1842. He would enjoy this new study only until 1882, the year of his death. It was during the forty years he spent in his old study that Darwin wrote the vast majority of his scientific papers and books. A wonderful example of the parents' forbearance was the stair slide that Charles and Emma had built for the children. It consisted of a wooden tray fastened at the top of the lower stairwell by a piece of wood that could be

Down House viewed from the garden side.

raised or lowered to change its angle. There was also a rope on the first-floor landing that could allow a child to swing out over the stairs. What parent today would indulge their children or condone the building of such a potentially head-cracking, arm-breaking apparatus?

The old study was chosen in part because of its northeast-facing direction, meaning that only a few beams of light could penetrate the room in the morning. His preferred place to write was in his high-backed armchair with a metal frame and wheels underneath to provide some mobility. While writing he used a foot cushion and he wrote on a board covered in cloth perched across the arms of the chair. The chair was in the northeast corner of the room near the window. To his right was an array of cupboards, drawers and multiple shelves on which he would place books and various notes he had made. Ever solicitous of his privacy, a mirror was later fitted outside between the two windows facing Luxted Road so that he might discern who was coming to the door before they knocked. On the far side of the fireplace was a drapery-covered corner, his personal privy, especially for the frequent times that he felt unwell. In the centre of the room was a substantial table that held books, papers or specimens upon which he happened to be working at the time. Between the windows facing Luxted Road was a revolving table upon which he could keep his current work in easy reach. His microscope was kept on a shelf by the right-hand window, furthest from his chair. Darwin's bookshelves filled the wall that was to the right as one walks into the room. Prominently positioned above the fireplace were portraits of Charles Lyell, Joseph Hooker and his maternal grandfather Josiah Wedgwood. As an indulgent father, his children often visited him in his study. Paper was not a common item, but Darwin allowed them to use scraps of paper for drawing. Some of these have been found to be from his original manuscript

Darwin's old study, Down House.

pages that he discarded after having a neat, exact copy made, known as a fair copy.

Over the years a number of structures and features were added to the grounds of Down House. They allowed Darwin to conduct various experiments in which his children acted first as helpers and then in later years as the editors and even co-authors of his resulting publications. He began his experiments on plants in the house's kitchen garden, but later had a greenhouse and hothouse built nearby specifically for this purpose. When he became involved in the breeding of pigeons to help him understand artificial selection he had an aviary built. Near the back of the house on the westerly lawn one can see today a large, circular stone with two metal rods protruding several centimetres from an opening in the middle. This is a replica of Darwin's worm stone that he used to mark the rate at which earthworms worked around the stone and gradually caused it to sink into the surrounding earth.

Certainly, one of the most famous and most recognized features of Down House is the Sandwalk. This elliptically elongate path is southwest of Down House on land first rented and then purchased from his neighbour John Lubbock. Various tree species were planted to encompass the path in a welcoming environment. Darwin regarded this as his thinking path. At its beginning he would place a line of small pebbles to be flicked away each time he completed a circuit. His usual habit was to complete a number of circuits on his morning and afternoon contemplative walks. The Sandwalk was held in some awe by his children and later grandchildren. They were both frightened and fascinated by a very large old beech on the path that in family lore was named the Elephant Tree because of its massive truncated branch which resembled the head of a great beast. Darwin's granddaughter and daughter of George, the wood engraver Gwen Raverat, never met her grandfather as she was born in 1885, three years after Darwin's death. She visited and had fond memories of Down House and gave

The Sandwalk, Down House, and the Elephant Tree.

the fullest account of the Elephant Tree in her memoir *Period Piece*, in which she describes and illustrates it with a 'monstrous head growing' from the trunk by day that changes into a 'monstrous ogre' by night.[2] More recently it was cut down because of disease and age, but a new one was planted to replace it.

After Charles Darwin's death at Down House in 1882 Emma bought a house in Cambridge called The Grove, where she lived with their daughter Elizabeth during the winter months. A main reason for her move to Cambridge was that three of her adult sons, Francis, George and Horace, lived there. She spent her summers at Down House, where she died in 1896. Into the early twentieth century various renters lived at Down House, but in 1907 it was turned into a girls' boarding school named Downe House School, which is still extant in Cold Ash, Berkshire, following its move there in 1922. This was followed by another, unidentified girls' school, run by a Miss Rain, but it closed in 1927. At the 1927 annual meeting of the British Association for the Advancement of Science (BAAS) an appeal was launched by Arthur Keith and George Buckston Browne to secure funds to purchase the home and property from the Darwin descendants. On 7 June 1929 a museum was opened under the auspices of BAAS.[3] For the next ten years the house and grounds were open to the public and admission was free. The property was closed during the Second World War and went through some harrowing times because of its proximity to the fighter base at Biggin Hill Airfield.[4] Following the war, owing to a lack of funding, ownership of Down House passed in 1953 to the Royal College of Surgeons, which minimally maintained the property until the Natural History Museum, London, and then English Heritage acquired the property in 1996 with the help of generous grants and trusts. The museum reopened two years later. Substantial renovations have been and continue to be undertaken at Down House, its outbuildings, the grounds and the gardens. Except for the museum areas that occupy parts of the interior spaces, attempts have been made to reconstruct as much as possible of the ground floor so that it resembles what Down House was like when the Darwin family occupied it more than 140 years ago.

Down House was not just a home for the Darwins, it would become their refuge and sanctuary from the later public scrutiny that came with Darwin's fame. They frequently entertained family, friends and colleagues, and although only a relatively short distance from central London some guests would stay the night, given the difficulty of travel in the early nineteenth century. One of the early friends Darwin made in Downe was Reverend John Brodie Innes. While it might seem out of character for Darwin to have developed what would be a life-long cordial correspondence with a local clergyman, their mutual interests began with the effort to help the less fortunate. Darwin and Innes were involved in the Coal and Clothing Fund, a local savings club. From 1848 through to 1869 Darwin made contributions to the fund, later taking over its running from Innes. The two also co-founded the Friendly Club, which requested contributions from locals to help assure assistance for those in need during difficult financial times. Darwin acted as secretary for the club for more than thirty years and often hosted the club's annual meeting at Down House. Innes shared Darwin's interest in natural history and their last correspondences in 1881, less than a year before Darwin's death, discussed bee and wasp behaviour and the shapes of their nests.

Early on Emma acted as translator for scientific papers in Italian, German and French as well as taking on the role of secretary to help organize Charles's affairs. She was instrumental in entertaining the many friends, colleagues and relatives who visited Down House, the number of which only grew over time along with Darwin's increasing fame. Emma often steered conversations with visitors towards politics because she enjoyed the topic and it took Charles's mind off his scientific pursuits. Emma also nursed Charles as he increasingly suffered debilitating illnesses that were exacerbated by his work. She would read to him, notably in the evenings and often from the family's favourite novels. On occasions when she could coax Charles away from Down House, she organized various family holidays to Wales, the Lake District and the Isle of Wight, as well as to the homes of relatives and friends. In Downe Emma helped to establish and supply a reading room for working men and ran a lending library for the local children. Emma was more devout than the creed of the Unitarian beliefs she was brought up in and so she involved herself with St Mary's Church, the local parish of the Church of England.

Even after moving to Down House, Darwin continued to visit London to attend various scientific society meetings. There he also had the opportunity to meet some of the best scientific minds of the day who came to London from around the world. He had already had many meetings with his early geological idol and mentor Charles Lyell, who resided in London. In early

January 1842 Darwin was able to finally meet the other great early idol and mentor he often wrote of in his voyage notebooks, Alexander von Humboldt, who was visiting the home of the British geologist Roderick Murchison. Darwin was no doubt flattered that the great man wished to meet him and had highly praised his *Narratives of the Voyage of the HMS Beagle*, but Darwin later remarked in his *Autobiography* that other than Humboldt being a 'very cheerful' man who 'talked too much', he could recall little of their discussion.[5]

While still living in London Darwin visited his older brother Ras. When Emma and Charles moved to Down House the latter frequently stayed with Ras when visiting London for scientific meetings. Ras had retired from medicine at the ripe old age of 26 because his health was deemed too poor to carry on with a medical career. In his rented rooms in London Ras's cosmopolitan life of leisure involved hosting dinner parties for literary figures, scientists and people often on the margins of acceptable politics. Among the latter was Harriet Martineau, social activist and theorist. His sisters had told Ras of Martineau in their letters. Ras and Harriet later became very close friends, often spending many of their days together. Their relationship generally suited most of the Darwin family, except that Martineau appeared to strongly dominate Ras. Their father Robert took a dimmer view of the relationship. Although himself a liberal Whig he found Martineau's politics far too radical for his tastes and thought her a poor match for Ras. He need not have worried, as they never married.

Although his scientific pursuits at the time buoyed his spirits, all was not well with the still young Darwin. Soon after his return from the voyage of the *Beagle*, he developed a host of health issues that were to plague him for the remainder of life, possibly even shortening it. As early as 1838 he complained of illness while working on his 'species theory'. Speculation is that his anxiety over such a controversial topic caused his illness. While plausibly part of his health complaints, there were other contributing factors, such as the continuing effects of Chagas disease, which he probably contracted from the bite of the vinchuca while in Argentina. He had even complained to his father of heart palpitations before the voyage – and we must not forget that he suffered near constant sea-sickness while at sea. All told, throughout his life Darwin reportedly suffered not only heart palpitations, but nervous exhaustion, tremors, vertigo, spasms, colic, bloating, flatulence, bouts of vomiting, headaches and skin problems. We do know that because of his severe facial eczema his wife Emma counselled him in 1862 to grow a beard, resulting in the famous visage we today imagine readily of the wise, contemplative scientist. As we shall see, in later intervals of his life he resorted to some rather unorthodox and quite suspect treatments to help alleviate his frequent suffering.

Darwin's book authorship kept a crisp pace in the early and mid-1840s. To his relief the monumental editorial supervision of *The Zoology of the Voyage of HMS Beagle* saw the final instalment published in 1843. Because of its popularity, Darwin began working on a second edition of his *Journal of Researches*. This appeared in 1845, published by John Murray and dedicated to Charles Lyell. The publication arrangement with John Murray would prove a very long and fruitful relationship for both parties as Murray became the primary publisher for twelve different books written by Darwin. The company had been founded in London in 1768 by John Murray, who was originally from Edinburgh. When his son John Murray II took over the business, he moved it to what would be the firm's long-term home at 50 Albemarle Street. It became an important centre for publishing as well as a gathering place for men of letters. What followed was a succession totalling seven John Murrays until the business was sold in 2002. It was John Murray III, grandson of the founder, with whom Darwin had a long-term working relationship that lasted more than 35 years.

The only other publishing house with whom Darwin regularly worked was Smith, Elder & Co., also of London. They published the three smaller volumes that complemented Darwin's narrative of the voyage. These were more technical treatments, and although republished at various times they never reached the popularity of his narratives. These three books were on coral reefs (1842), volcanic islands (1844) and South American geology (1846). It was the first of these that had the most lasting impact and is today best known. In it he argued that ring-shaped coral atolls form around volcanic islands. As islands erode below the waves, the corals continue to grow upwards to stay within the zone where sunlight can reach, thus providing the atoll's ring-like form.

In 1842 Darwin took the next step beyond his notebooks on evolution by completing a 35-page essay laying out his then nascent ideas. For some time after his death in 1882 it was thought that this 'pencil sketch' had been lost. Fortunately for us, after Emma's death in 1896 the essay was found in a cupboard below the stairs at Down House. By the early 1840s Darwin's work on the 'species question' was becoming an open secret among his friends. Charles Lyell was touring the United States in 1842 when he became aware that Darwin was musing over the species question. Lyell was none too receptive. In 1844 Darwin wrote a longer version that came in at 230 pages in which he provided the fullest explanations to date of his work on descent with modification by means of natural selection. He asked Emma to arrange for publication of this larger essay in the event of his death. He asked her to seek out a person capable of enlarging, improving and publishing it, setting aside £400 for this purpose. For this editorial task he specifically identified his geological mentor Charles Lyell, the naturalist Edward Forbes, his Cambridge mentor John Henslow, his botanical friend and colleague J. D. Hooker, the naturalist Hugh Strickland and the anatomist Richard Owen. He later wisely deleted Owen because of increasing animosity between the two men and in pencil wrote on the cover of the essay that Joseph D. Hooker was by far the best man to edit his essay. In January 1844 Darwin wrote to Hooker, coyly stating he was almost convinced that species were not immutable with the caveat that this was tantamount to confessing to murder. He later provided Hooker with a copy of the longer essay. Although supportive of Darwin's work on the topic, Hooker remained unconvinced of transmutation, especially with natural selection as a mechanism.

An event that occurred in 1844 shook Darwin's confidence and prudence with regard to the species question. This was the anonymous publication of *Vestiges of Creation*. It combined various ideas on the evolution of the stars, as well as of organisms on Earth by a progressive transmutation of species. The work was a true Victorian sensation, appealing not just to English radicals but to the public at large, with Prince Albert reportedly reading it to Queen Victoria. Whereas the public found *Vestiges* scandalous but fascinating, scientific reviews savaged it and called the speculations within unsubstantiated. When Darwin read it, he was relieved that none of his arguments concerning evolution, notably natural selection, were apparent. More to the point, in a letter to Hooker he indicated that 'I have, also, read the Vestiges, but have been somewhat less amused at it, than you appear to have been: the writing & arrangement are certainly admirable, but his geology strikes me as bad, & his zoology far worse.'[6] Although critical, Darwin recognized that the publication of *Vestiges* helped to pave the way for his own work and indicated a sea change in public opinion regarding the evolution of species. There was speculation as to the identity of the work's anonymous author, but it was not until the publication of the twelfth edition in 1884 that the Scottish publisher Robert Chambers, who had died in 1871, was revealed as the author.

The year after *Vestiges* appeared, 1845, brought Darwin even more profound concerns and was the start of what would prove to be a major shift in his work for the next eight years. Hooker had read the longer 1844 essay on the species question that Darwin gave to him and he remarked in a letter to Darwin in autumn 1845 that one should not theorize on a grander scale in biology without having done a detailed taxonomic study involving hundreds of species from around the globe.[7] Hooker claimed that he was not specifically targeting Darwin for his theorizing, but Darwin nonetheless took this admonishment to heart, beginning what would become his most detailed study of a specific group – barnacles. His dive into the cryptic world of barnacle anatomy, reproduction and classification would consume him from 1846 to 1854, during which time he toiled and wrote, resulting in a four-volume monographic study that is still highly regarded today. This consumed much of Darwin's time and efforts, yet he was steadily working on the species question that he came to call his 'big book'.

6

Where Does He Do His Barnacles?

Intended or not, Joseph Hooker's admonishment that one first must undertake a detailed taxonomic study before proposing grand biological theories struck home with Darwin. If not the only catalyst, Hooker's counsel certainly played a role in the next eight-year study Darwin undertook on the lowly barnacle.

Why did Darwin choose this obscure yet fascinating group to study? Until the early nineteenth century, barnacles, known formally as Cirripedia, were thought to belong among the Mollusca, the group that includes octopuses, snails and clams, because as with some of this group the sedentary bodies of barnacles are encased in a multipart shell. Then in the 1830s research on the metamorphosis from larva to adult showed they are more closely related to crustaceans, the group that includes lobsters, crabs and shrimp. From correspondence we know that Darwin had been particularly taken by a single species of barnacle he had encountered in Chile that often burrowed in the shells of other marine vertebrates. He anthropomorphized it as 'Mr Arthrobalanus', meaning articulated Balanus, but later formally named it *Cryptophialus minutus.* More broadly Darwin saw this as a very fertile area of study because little was known and what was known was poorly done. A massive study of barnacles by Darwin would not only demonstrate his seriousness as a taxonomically based naturalist but aid in his broader quest pertaining to how species change.

Darwin never did anything half-heartedly. He plunged into the study of not just some, but all barnacles. He had gathered a number of interesting examples while on the *Beagle*, but as he did with other projects, he posted well over three hundred letters to friends and colleagues regarding barnacles, many requesting specimens of both living and extinct species. These specimens included not only preserved examples of living species, but fossils as well. This was to include all species of Cirripedia, living and extinct, that he could acquire. Soon his study room and other parts of Down House overflowed with specimens he had obtained from Britain and beyond, sometimes to the consternation of those around him. Darwin became so fully absorbed in the research that his young son George apparently thought that every father studied barnacles, asking at a friend's home where in the house the boy's father studied his barnacles.

A lot of time was spent dissecting and describing the anatomy of the preserved specimens under a microscope. Darwin was no stranger to this scientific instrument. In May 1831, as he finished as a student at Cambridge, he received, anonymously, a hand-held Coddington-designed microscope probably built by the London instrument makers George and John Cary. Darwin later learned that the thoughtful gift had come from John M. Herbert, a university friend and lifelong correspondent.[1] On the *Beagle* voyage he extensively used a small, low-powered microscope. The work he was now undertaking on barnacles involved long hours in which he would constantly peer down a microscope, day in and day out, meaning that he required not only the simpler microscopes that he still used, but a more sophisticated instrument. In 1846 he had James Smith build a monocular achromatic microscope. This newer achromatic lens was built in such a way that it helped to limit the effects of colour and shape aberrations. This was important as Darwin tried to differentiate subtle differences in the parts of the small creatures he was studying. The microscope had an impressive

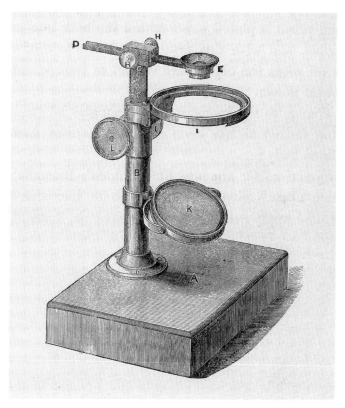

One kind of microscope used by Darwin.

lens capable of considerable magnification, but for his bits and pieces of barnacles the best-quality image was perhaps no more than about 800× magnification. He would go on to use this kind of microscope in the coming years for his detailed work on plants, even after newer models became available.

Darwin discovered and traced the eggs from within the base of barnacles as they developed through the larval stage into adults, confirming the view that barnacles are crustaceans and not molluscs. His research revealed other fascinating aspects of barnacle biology. Because of the manner in which they seemed to reproduce, it was thought that barnacles were hermaphrodites – that is, that a single barnacle was both male and female. Darwin showed that in some species males had evolved from independent living forms to much simpler, minute, mostly sperm-producing entities living on the body of the female. He also found that the oviduct, the egg-laying organ of other crustaceans, had been modified in barnacles to release adhesive secretions that allowed the developing larva to attach to its desired substrate such as a rock or a ship's hull. These studies helped Darwin to better understand the complexity of biological nomenclature and provided a specific case for studying the species question. Although he never wrote specifically regarding the evolutionary history of barnacles, his classification of these marine species certainly reflected their evolutionary past. Even 160 years later, Darwin's barnacle work is still consulted.

On 13 November 1848, in the midst of his study of barnacles, Darwin learned from his sister Emily Catherine that their father Robert Waring Darwin had died at The Mount, Shrewsbury.[2] Darwin knew that his father's death was imminent as he had visited The Mount the month before, finding him gravely ill and greatly changed, as one might expect from such a large figure now reduced to a failing body. Although the funeral was to be held several days after Charles learned of his father's death, he did not arrive in Shrewsbury in time to attend. Darwin was unwell and stayed at The Mount with his sister Marianne, who also was too unwell to attend her father's funeral. Not attending his father's funeral was indicative of a pattern for Darwin. He could not bring himself three years later, in 1851, to attend the burial of his beloved first daughter, ten-year-old Annie, either. He also would not attend the funeral in 1861 of his great Cambridge tutor John Stevens Henslow. Henslow, who suffered with heart problems, became very ill in the winter of 1860. Many visitors, such as J. D. Hooker, came to stand vigil and bid him farewell, but Darwin was conspicuously absent. Yes, Darwin's own health was poor at the time, yet it remains curious that he stayed away. One can only surmise that it was not out of callousness but from an inability to deal with the deaths of those to whom he had been close – a father, a daughter and a mentor.

Darwin's ever-present ailments were aggravated by his intense, often-tedious barnacle work. He sought a new treatment. He settled on the 'water cure' of Dr James Gully in the spa town of Great Malvern, Worcestershire, some 210 kilometres (130 mi.) northwest of Down House. Darwin rented a large house in Malvern and took his growing family there in March 1849 for a two-month stay. By this time their sixth child, Elizabeth, and seventh, Francis, had increased the Darwin brood to six living children (with the death of the infant Mary Eleanor in 1842). While the family was otherwise occupied in the environs of Great Malvern, Darwin endured a strict regime of having his body heated with spirit lamps, robust rubdowns with cold wet towels, foot baths in cold water, walks and a strict diet. Darwin continued the water cure sporadically at Down House, where he had a cold-water shower built behind his home. His manservant Joseph Parslow aided in the management of the shower. Darwin also took walks on his beloved Sandwalk, usually twice daily, as part of the regime. It provided an escape to contemplate his work as well as to exercise.

Visits continued on and off for three years to Malvern with a tragic turn of events there in 1851. The Darwins' oldest daughter Annie, along with her sisters Elizabeth and Henrietta, had been dealing with complications of scarlet fever since late 1849. By early 1851, still suffering from its aftermath, Henrietta and Annie were taken to Malvern to see if the water cure programme might help alleviate their symptoms. On a second visit to Malvern on 16 April Annie, Charles's favourite child, died of complications resulting from either scarlet fever or tuberculosis and other health issues. She was buried in Great Malvern, but Darwin did not attend the funeral. Life would not stand still; Annie's death had been bookended by the birth of Charles's eighth child, Leonard, in 1850 and then a ninth child, Horace, in 1851, less than a month following Annie's death. Darwin did not return to Malvern for twelve years, mostly owing to the painful memory of Annie's death there. He did seek hydropathic treatments intermittently over the next ten years at Moor Park in Surrey and Ilkley in Yorkshire, with only

Anne 'Annie' Elizabeth Darwin, 1849.

temporary relief. Although such treatments were fashionable in Victorian England, they had their detractors, and Darwin always showed great scepticism towards Dr Gully's other beliefs in clairvoyance and homeopathy. Even more importantly, his religious views and belief in a personal God had been waning for some years, and after Annie's death the last vestiges of these beliefs died for Darwin. He still helped to support the community work of his local parish, but even before Annie's death he would accompany his family only towards the church, not inside it, preferring to take a Sunday walk outdoors.

The barnacle work helped to focus Darwin on something other than his losses. Diversions helped. In the year 1851 the Great Exhibition of the Works of Industry of All Nations, the brainchild of Queen Victoria's husband Prince Albert and Henry Cole, the British inventor and civil servant, was held in Hyde Park. The exhibition space was the immense structure of plate glass and cast iron that earned the nickname the Crystal Palace. The use of the relatively newly developed method of making large sheets of plate glass permitted such a grandiose structure, amazing all who saw it. The structure, at around 92,000 square metres (almost 1 million sq. ft), housed 14,000 exhibitions from around the world. The entire Darwin family, with the newborn Horace in tow, availed themselves of this once-in-a-lifetime spectacle by going to London to stay with Charles's brother Ras in his new home on Park Street in late July and early August with Darwin making a solo return visit also in early August. After the exhibition the Crystal Palace, which was intentionally built to be a temporary structure, was dismantled and rebuilt in 1854 in Bromley, a south London borough. Charles and Emma purchased season tickets for the Crystal Palace, attending its opening in June of that year. The Crystal Palace was destroyed by fire in 1936, but Benjamin Waterhouse Hawkins's delightfully anachronistic dinosaur reconstructions, made for the rebuilt palace, survive to this day.

The 1851 Great Exhibition held in Hyde Park, London.

The reconstructions include not just the more famous dinosaurs but also lesser-known mammals, including the ground sloth *Megatherium*, bones of which Darwin found in South America.

During the eight years of barnacle research of 1846–54 Darwin needed to make time for other tasks. In 1845 he had commenced work on the second edition of what was then known by the shortened title *Journal of Researches*. Some of his later books would also see additional press runs and even new editions depending on the book's popularity. In 1846 Darwin also finished and published the last of his three more technical books on the geology of his earlier voyage, *Geological Observations on South America*. He also frequently travelled to attend scientific meetings during these years. This was in spite of his often-debilitating mélange of illnesses, which he noted in 1854 had cumulatively cost him a year in completing his work on barnacles. It is thus remarkable what he could and did accomplish. Darwin belonged to and participated in a host of scientific societies. In 1837 he had joined the council of the Geological Society of London and in 1838 he reluctantly became its secretary, a role which he later resigned from, mostly due to his health. He remained for some time on the council and regularly attended its meetings in London throughout the year. These were not the only meetings he joined both in London and around England. He also appeared at meetings of the British Association for the Advancement of Science, the Royal Society and the Linnean Society, sometimes accompanied by Emma.

In 1851, the same year as Annie's death, Darwin could see the culmination of his toils on barnacles beginning to bear fruit. The first of two slim volumes on fossil barnacles was published by the Palaeontographical Society and the first of two more massive tomes on living barnacles was published by the Ray Society. Both volumes dealt with lepadid or stalked barnacles. These works were followed in 1854 by the second volumes of both fossil and living balanid or sessile barnacles. Before this second set of volumes appeared, Darwin was receiving praise for his barnacle work. In 1853 Darwin had been awarded the Royal Medal of the Royal Society for his work on barnacles as well as on corals, volcanic islands and the geology of South America. It wasn't until 1890, after his death, that the Royal Society established the Darwin Medal to recognize 'distinction in evolution, population biology, organismal biology and biological diversity'. Fittingly its first recipient was Alfred

Russel Wallace, who in 1858 had been the co-discoverer of natural selection along with Darwin.

The year 1854 was one of honours for Darwin. He received more recognition from the Royal Society when on 24 April he was elected to the Philosophical Club, an elite club within the Royal Society. The Philosophical Club was reportedly established in 1743, ostensibly for certain members of the Royal Society to assemble and dine together. At this time its membership included younger scientists and others open to newer ideas, so the club would have appealed to Darwin while he was still developing his theory of species' origins. Over the next half a dozen years Darwin regularly attended gatherings of the Philosophical Club, often in conjunction with Royal Society meetings. Darwin was also recognized by the Linnean Society when that same year they made him a Fellow. This society was founded in 1788, taking its name from the Swedish naturalist Carl von Linné (Linnaeus), the father of modern biological taxonomy and classification. It is the oldest existing natural history society in the world. Darwin would be further immortalized by the Linnean Society when in 1908 it established the Darwin-Wallace Medal to reward major advances in evolutionary biology. The first gold medal, as with the inaugural Darwin Medal eighteen years previously, went to Alfred Russel Wallace.

Although nothing about species change was stated in the barnacle monographs, it is still evident that the taxonomic arrangements used by Darwin were intended to show what he thought of the group's evolutionary history, notably the deep taxonomic divisions between the lepadid or stalked barnacles and the balanid or sessile barnacles that reflected their long, separate histories. He strongly believed that classifications should reflect this history. If he had directly mentioned the mutability of species in his barnacle work it is highly unlikely that he would have received such accolades and awards as the Royal Medal of the Royal

Society, election to the Philosophical Club, or be elected a Fellow of the Linnean Society. Science and society were not quite ready, yet four years later Darwin set before them his very cogent arguments of the mutability of species.

The importance of Darwin's barnacle work remains to the present day. He had fulfilled Hooker's dictum to complete a comprehensive taxonomic study before tackling far-reaching theoretical matters, namely his ever-present exploration of the species question. Yet we can forgive Darwin his proclamation in a letter to his cousin William Darwin Fox that after seeing the work to completion, 'I hate a Barnacle as no man ever did before, not even a Sailor in a slow-sailing ship.'[3] In September 1854, with his barnacle work complete, Darwin packed up all of his specimens and recorded in his diary that he could now return to sorting his notes for his species theory. He could now expend most of his energy on his 'big book'. His work on barnacles had not been a digression but rather one more piece of the cumulative process of gathering facts, data and information to eventually make evolutionary theorizing one long, strongly supported argument. Darwin now understood how doing detailed specimen descriptions was key to building his theoretical ideas on the origins and changes in species over time. Hooker's earlier admonition had paid dividends.

7

Lyell's Words Come True with a Vengeance

Barnacles had consumed Darwin for the past eight years and the death of his beloved Annie had weighed on him heavily. Now, however, he needed renewed focus in returning to the species question that he had first pondered in his 1837 notebook. In the years following the *Beagle* voyage Darwin had amassed many pages on varied subjects, such as artificial and natural selection, hybridization, variation and its causes, the fossil record, and plant and animal distributions. His energy and attention were required to put them into some sort of order. Although his theorizing began privately in his notebooks, it did not remain that way for very long. Through his correspondence and comments to family, friends and colleagues it is clear that they knew of his work on the species question, but what was unclear was how much more detail he dared to share with them. His wife Emma certainly knew of his work when in 1844 Darwin had asked her to publish his larger essay on the species question in the event of his death.

Darwin guardedly began to broach the subject of mutability of species with his geological mentor Charles Lyell. In September 1838, near the end of a very long letter to Lyell, Darwin had written almost in passing, 'I have lately been . . . concerned, by the delightful number of new views, which have been coming in, thickly & steadily, on the classification & affinities & instincts of animals – bearing on the question of species – note book, after note book has been filled, with facts, which begin to group themselves *clearly* under sub-laws.'[1] To our minds there is no mistaking Darwin's intent in this passage, yet it only expresses to Lyell his great fascination for the topic. It was certainly not yet time to share the heretical content of these notebooks. Although lukewarm on the veracity of evolution, in part because of his religious beliefs, over the years Lyell increasingly urged Darwin to place his ideas before the public and scientific communities. While in South America on the *Beagle* voyage Darwin obtained the second volume of Lyell's *Principles of Geology*. In it, Lyell rejected Lamarck's ideas on evolution but nevertheless found the arguments a courageous effort. This informs us about Lyell's character in that although he may not have agreed with a particular theoretical premise, if soundly argued he believed strongly it should see the light of day, certainly a trait carried over from his background in the law. Lyell had argued for an immensely old and very stable Earth and for the fact that extinctions occurred – ideas that were still not wholly accepted in the early nineteenth century. Darwin fully embraced both ideas while onboard the *Beagle,* even if he later quibbled with Lyell as to how and why extinctions took place. Lyell argued that the majority of extinctions were caused by changing environmental conditions, whereas Darwin more and more came to believe that most extinctions occurred when species failed in competition with other, often descendant species. Thus for Lyell it was a physical cause while for Darwin it was a biological cause. As these processes are not mutually exclusive, both men were at least partially correct.

The question for Lyell, and of course others, was not necessarily how species became extinct, but rather how new species have arisen. The answer to the latter query can be found preserved in the fossil record in different parts of the world. Lyell answered this in the second volume of *Principles* by proposing what he termed

'Centres of Creation' for the appearance of new forms in different regions – not by evolution but thorough divine intervention. He came close here to accepting some form of natural change in species over time, even if divinely inspired. When Lyell became increasingly aware of Darwin's work through correspondence, meetings and eventually reading parts of Darwin's 'big book', Lyell slowly became a more receptive if not an accepting audience as Darwin shared the accumulating proof for evolution.

It was in January 1844, prior to asking Emma to publish his essay on evolution of species by means of natural selection if he should die unexpectedly, that Darwin had written to the slightly younger botanist J. D. Hooker. In his correspondence with Hooker, Darwin posited the view that species were not immutable. Although only a recent acquaintance, perhaps Darwin sensed in Hooker a person open and receptive to his ideas. In 1847, convinced that Hooker would give his ideas a fair hearing, Darwin provided the botanist with a copy of his 1844 essay during a visit to Down House.[2] Although supportive of Darwin's work on the topic, Hooker for the time being remained unconvinced of the mutability of species, especially with natural selection as the mechanism. (Recall that it was Hooker's caution in 1845 that one should not theorize before completing a detailed taxonomic study that set Darwin on his eight-year barnacle sojourn that in the end gave Darwin more ammunition for his theory.)

In 1839 Hooker introduced Darwin to the American botanist Asa Gray while Gray was visiting Kew Gardens, London. Only a year younger than Darwin, Gray became the first botany professor and head of the Botanic Garden at Harvard College in 1842. It was not until 1855 that the two began an extensive correspondence. Darwin was at first especially interested in what Gray could tell him about the distribution of American flowering plants as such data could add to the growing body of evidence Darwin was using to show how plant and animal distributions made sense in the

Asa Gray, famed American botanist, colleague and good friend of Darwin, 1855.

light of evolution. Then in 1857 Darwin took the gamble of sending Gray a copy of his 1844 essay.[3] Gray eventually became the earliest champion of Darwin's ideas in the United States when they were published two years later, but Gray argued that a creator had directed evolutionary change, something that Darwin did not countenance.

A number of other people were aware at some level of the evolutionary theorizing in which Darwin was engaged. It was, however, Lyell, Hooker and Gray who knew most about the work and acted as honest brokers in helping Darwin hone his ideas and arguments. In the process Darwin convinced each of these three men to accept the likelihood that species did change or evolve over long periods of time by means of natural selection. Lyell remained the most reluctant of these three scientists and the last to accept natural selection, if he eventually did somewhat tepidly. None of these scientists fully accepted all of Darwin's arguments, yet to their great credit all of them pressed Darwin to publish his ideas before someone else beat him to it. In the end it was through the indirect results of correspondence with Gray and the direct actions of Lyell and Hooker that Darwin's evolutionary theory would first be presented publicly in 1858.

Another scientist who would later become an important vocal champion of Darwin's cause was Thomas Henry Huxley, sixteen years Darwin's junior, who was also a good friend of Hooker. Darwin found Huxley a pugnacious, direct-spoken scientist who did not suffer fools lightly and who was ready to take on all comers with whom he disagreed. He would also prove to be the best English comparative anatomist in the latter half of the nineteenth century. Even though an iconoclast of sorts, Huxley opposed the idea that species evolved, having been an ardent critic of the anonymously published *Vestiges of Creation* of 1844. Darwin had also been a critic of *Vestiges*, but unlike Huxley he opposed it because of its lack of scientific rigour, not because of its support of evolution, which was his still-discrete passionate enquiry at the time, shared only with a few people such as Hooker.

Darwin and Huxley had met in 1851 shortly after the latter's return from the surveying voyage of HMS *Rattlesnake* to New Guinea and Australia in 1846–50. Huxley had served as a surgeon's mate and naturalist of marine life on the voyage, making his and Darwin's shared experiences of long voyages as a naturalist and work on marine animals both clear points of common interest. Huxley's foray into work on medusae, the free-swimming sexual form of jellyfishes, corals and their relatives, was published in 1849, providing scientific recognition for the young scientist. Because of their common interests, Darwin was able to cajole Huxley into reviewing his published barnacle work. As Hooker had argued, Darwin's barnacle monographs would place him among the ranks of competent taxonomists and thus give Darwin's theoretical work on evolution more credence when it was finally revealed to the

Thomas Henry Huxley, famed English anatomist, *c.* 1861.

public. Huxley obliged Darwin by extensively praising his barnacle monographs in a lecture on the topic published in 1857.[4]

Darwin had now lined up a number of colleagues and friends who either knew or would soon know of his work on the question of species mutability. What proved to be a seminal dinner occurred on 26 April 1856 at Down House. On the several days preceding and after the dinner, the Darwins hosted Huxley and his wife Henrietta, Hooker and his wife Frances (the daughter of Henslow), as well as the entomologist Thomas Vernon Wollaston. The Darwins also invited their young friend and neighbour John Lubbock and his new wife Ellen to dine with the assembled group. By all accounts the conversation ranged widely and wildly on scientific matters, including the mutability of species, and it continued over the next few days. A major motive of Darwin's was certainly to sound out these probably sympathetic colleagues on his heretical ideas on transmutation of species, providing more detail than he heretofore had disclosed. Having been privy to much of the argumentation for more than ten years after reading Darwin's 1844 essay, Hooker knew more than the others of Darwin's supposition. The others

Middle-aged Charles and Emma with son Leonard, *c.* 1853.

would soon learn more. It would be only Wollaston that for religious reasons would later become a critic of Darwin's version of evolution yet had himself argued for a limited form of species changes, particularly on islands.

Although Lyell did not attend this conclave he heard of its boisterous scientific musings and was already aware of how far Darwin had matured in his theorizing.[5] While at Down House in early April Darwin explained to Lyell in some detail the contents of his 'big book' and how large the manuscript had grown. Although troubled by what Darwin was proposing he could see how it eclipsed Lamarck's ideas and argumentation. Darwin explained to Lyell that he wished to publish his 'big book' as a large, complete work titled *Natural Selection*. Lyell countered that Darwin should prepare and publish a much shorter version before someone else published the same ideas first. Although Darwin considered Lyell's proposal of a shortened sketch, he eventually rejected it and continued to intensively work on the much larger manuscript for the remainder of 1856 into early 1858. Some of chapters included topics he named geographical distribution, natural variation, struggle for existence, natural selection, hybridism, instinct and divergence. By mid-April 1858 the intensity of the work and probably the emotional strain took its toll on his health, leading Darwin to resort to an old remedy, hydropathy, though he now chose to attend a closer facility some 65 kilometres (40 mi.) away at Moor Park in Farnham. He complained that this illness cost him a month or more of work.

During this busy time Darwin managed to continue some of his experimental work at Down House. It undoubtedly provided a needed respite from working on his 'big book'. He also spoke with various farmers and breeders about their practices in choosing desirable traits, becoming so interested that he set up a breeding programme for domestic pigeons at Down House. His father had kept birds at The Mount when Charles was young, so he had some idea of what was involved. He was also aware of the popularity at the time of raising the fifteen or so fancy pigeon breeds and the information that could be gleaned about variations and inherited traits from dealing with breeders. To this end he had an aviary built at Down House in 1856 so that he might perform breeding experiments. This was not purely scientific, as he enjoyed the camaraderie of other breeders. Whereas the bird fanciers thought their different breeds descended from various wild stocks, scientists thought they descended from one – the position that Darwin took. This was important to the ideas he posited in his own research as it provided evidence of how the many pigeon breeds descended from one ancestor by artificially selecting individuals over many generations. It would not be a great leap to argue that in the natural world plants and animals had similarly descended from a common ancestry through a process akin to artificial selection that he named 'natural selection'.

Pigeons were not the only birds that Darwin experimented upon at Down House. He devised several experiments in which he enlisted his children to better learn how various species, especially those that could not fly, might be passively transported to distant places such as the Galápagos Islands. In one experiment he obtained three tablespoons of mud from the margin of a nearby pond. The five hundred plants he grew from these samples included a number of species. He hypothesized that based on this it was likely that water could transport seeds passively and that shore birds could actively transport such seeds on their feet or in their guts as they flew considerable distances. In another experiment he suspended duck's feet in his aquarium, which contained eggs, larvae and adults of small, shelled freshwater creatures. Some of the very small just-hatched creatures survived on the duck's feet for up to twenty hours in moist air. Darwin pointed out that in this time a heron or duck could fly at least 965 or 1,130 kilometres (600–700 mi.) before alighting on another pond.

As usual, various aspects of family life continued apace at Down House during this intense time for Darwin. Following the custom of the time for people of Darwin's social class, as the five Darwin sons each in their turn began to mature, they went off to boarding school while the two surviving daughters were schooled closer to home. The oldest Darwin child, William, was the first to go, attending Rugby School, Warwickshire, and from there Christ's College, University of Cambridge. After university he took a position with a bank in Southampton, where he remained. William was a great advocate for higher education for all and he was instrumental in the establishment of what would become the University of Southampton. He married an American, Sara Price Ashburner Sedgwick. They had no children, but he became a favourite of his nieces. As the eldest, he frequently hosted visits from his father, mother and the rest of the Darwin family in Southampton.

William had been the first child born to Emma and Charles in 1839. When William was already seventeen years old, the tenth and last Darwin child, whom they named Charles Waring Darwin, was born on 6 December 1856. Within the year it was realized that he had developmental issues, notably in walking and talking, which based on descriptions by family members are consistent with Down syndrome. Since Emma and Darwin were first cousins, he had always been concerned about the possible ramifications of inbreeding for their offspring. While there is a slightly increased risk of inherited physical or learning disabilities with children of first-cousin marriages, it was the fact of Emma being 48 years old at the time of Charles Waring's birth that was the greater risk factor for Down syndrome.

In mid-June 1858 Darwin was organizing some of his work on pigeons when in the post arrived a packet containing a letter and handwritten essay by Alfred Russel Wallace.[6] It probably had been posted in March from Ternate in the Moluccas, then part of the

Dutch East Indies, now Indonesia. It had taken until June for the correspondence to reach Darwin. In 1856 Lyell had recommended to Darwin an 1855 paper by Wallace, 'On the Law Which Has Regulated the Introduction of New Species', because it touched on some of the same questions Darwin tackled in his own species work. By the time he recommended Wallace's paper to Darwin, Lyell had learned the true extent of Darwin's species work. Lyell felt that Wallace's paper was a harbinger of other scientists publishing on the species problem before Darwin could do so. Another colleague in India, Edward Blyth, innocently wrote to Darwin saying that this Wallace paper made a convincing argument as to how domestic species had diverged to form new species.[7]

Wallace later recounted that Darwin and he had briefly met at the British Museum before Wallace's departure to the Malay archipelago in 1854, but Darwin could not recollect the encounter. They did correspond in 1857, however, to discuss species succession, variation and distribution. In these letters Darwin even mentioned to Wallace how some twenty years earlier he had opened his first notebook on species variation and on the question of how species and varieties differ one from another.[8] Neither Wallace's 1855 paper nor their 1857 correspondence sufficiently concerned Darwin as he thought he detected nothing new in Wallace's writings. With the arrival of this latest letter and essay from Wallace, Darwin was about to learn the full extent of his lapse of judgement and how correct Lyell's advice to publish had been.

As Darwin opened the packet and read Wallace's handwritten essay, he became more and more stricken by what he saw; Lyell's warning had come painfully true. The essay, written in February 1858 while Wallace was in Ternate, was titled 'On the Tendency of Varieties to Depart Indefinitely from the Original Type'. Wallace presented what on first blush seemed to be Darwin's theory of descent with modification by means of natural selection as if he had been reading the mind of Darwin as he wrote. Wallace

Alfred Russel Wallace, English co-discoverer of natural selection, *c.* 1895.

even incorporated Malthus's thesis on population growth, just as Darwin had done twenty years earlier to explain the process of natural selection. Darwin felt that his twenty years of painstakingly building a scientific edifice had just crumbled to dust right before him. The accompanying letter asked Darwin to pass the manuscript along to Lyell to see if he thought it worthy of publication. Wallace had written to Darwin in all innocence, knowing that he was interested in the species question but having no idea that Darwin had amassed evidence on the issue over the past twenty years. He asked Darwin to be the go-between with Lyell because he and Darwin had corresponded, and he probably felt awkward about directly approaching the august geologist. Although devastated, Darwin felt it would be unethical to rush to publish simply to claim priority; his honour was at stake. Perhaps he remembered, even if unconsciously, his experience many years before at the University of Edinburgh when Robert Edmond Grant had not properly credited Darwin for his discovery of new marine organisms.

Even in his angst Darwin dutifully sent along Wallace's essay to Lyell on 18 June.[9] In his letter he wrote that Lyell's predictions about another author pre-empting his theory had come true with a vengeance. He wrote that his originality had been smashed, but hoped that all the many years of work would still have value when his book was published. He had been operating with blinders in place, assuming that no one else could possibly arrive at his conclusions, even when his colleagues warned him to hasten his pace of publication. They knew that conjectures on evolution were being blown about by the intellectual winds.

Lyell responded immediately by letter that Darwin should prepare a short sketch of his theory for publication, but Darwin would have none of what he regarded as a dishonourable course of action.[10] He appealed to Lyell to contact Hooker, his great friend and evolutionary confidant, to wrestle with what might be done in this seemingly intractable situation. Within a few days Darwin received word from them about what seemed to be a solution to this conundrum – publish jointly. In this way both authors would receive credit for discovering the theory of evolution by means of natural selection, but by choosing one or more of Darwin's earlier manuscripts it would be clear that he had been working on the topic for some time. History has sometimes been unkind in viewing this solution as underhanded. But the proposal allowed both authors to receive equal billing and credit in keeping with the work each had done to date. Wallace would of course know nothing of the publication of a joint paper, as notification of the publication would take months to reach him in the Malay archipelago. The best course of action was to present the joint paper as soon as possible. It was decided that the meeting of the Linnean Society due in only a week on 1 July seemed the most expeditious solution for a place to have the joint paper read. Another issue prompted this urgency. Wallace of course had sent his letter and essay manuscript to Darwin for transmittal to Lyell. In order to ensure that at least one copy of his manuscript reach England, perhaps Wallace had sent another copy to an additional correspondent. This was not the case, but there was no way for Darwin and his supporters to know this at the time. Thus, time was perceived to be of the essence.

Wallace's essay served as an important catalyst for Darwin. Instead of his continuing to slog away at what would be a multi-volume 'big book' to be completed some years in the future, Darwin now set about completing a single volume that would be published in just over one year. He could not know then that this single book would capture the imagination of the public and of science more than any longer multi-volume tome could have done. On 20 June 1858 Darwin commenced what he now called the 'abstract' of his work, but the fates were not looking kindly on Darwin. He was now confronted with another crisis, this one concerning his family. Their fifteen-year-old daughter Henrietta came down with a high temperature and a terrible sore throat and then baby Darwin also developed a fever that simply would not abate. Thus, Darwin faced emergencies on two fronts, seemingly with little way forward. In the midst of the wrangling over which of Darwin's manuscripts to include in the presentation of the joint paper, baby Darwin died, leaving the whole family deeply bereft. In his grief and in no state to decide himself, Darwin sent Hooker unpublished material from which the latter could select pieces to include in the joint paper.[11] In the end Hooker chose both of the items that Darwin sent. First was a summary of the 1844 essay that Hooker had already read and an abstract of an 1857 letter to Asa Gray laying out Darwin's theory. This would then be followed by Wallace's essay.

The paper titled 'On the Tendency of Species to form Varieties; and on the Perpetuation of Varieties and Species by Natural Means of Selection' identified both Darwin and Wallace as the authors, and Lyell and Hooker wrote an introductory letter, all of which were read aloud by the society secretary John Joseph Bennett at the meeting on 1 July. There was only muted interest in the reading of the paper, which appeared in print in the *Zoological Journal of the Linnean Society* on 20 August. The president of the society, Thomas Bell, who presided at the meeting, wrote in his annual report in May 1859 that no 'striking discoveries' had occurred the previous year – the statement probably a result of his disapproval of the joint paper. He certainly knew the principals involved. He had described the reptiles and amphibians in *The Zoology of the Voyage of HMS Beagle* twenty years earlier for Darwin.

Neither author was present at the momentous but unheralded July meeting. Darwin was at Down House grieving the loss of his eighteen-month-old son and Wallace was far away in Asia, totally oblivious to the proceedings taking place in England. Some have claimed that the actions of Darwin, Lyell and Hooker were a nefarious plot to rob Wallace of his rightful place as the originator of evolution by means of natural selection. One can argue the merits of the course that this trio eventually decided upon, but in his actions, public statements and correspondence Wallace always claimed to be very pleased with sharing the honour as co-discoverer of natural selection. This might be best summed up by Wallace's dedication of his 1869 book *The Malay Archipelago* to Darwin in which he noted his 'personal esteem and friendship' and his 'deep admiration for his genius and his works'. He also published a book in 1889 titled *Darwinism*. Both these actions are very unlikely to have been done if he had felt slighted by Darwin and his compatriots.

Although their friendship would grow over the years, it is no surprise that there were to be differences between the two gifted men. Wallace urged Darwin to replace 'natural selection' with 'survival of the fittest', a term proposed by Herbert Spencer, because to Wallace the phrase 'natural selection' implied a selector. Darwin did not abandon natural selection but did oblige Wallace by using Spencer's phrase in the fifth edition of *On the Origin of Species*, published in 1869. Over the years this phrase has proved an unfortunate alternative, because there has been much confusion over what is meant by 'fitness'. In the vernacular, fitness implies strength, and in this instance, it would be strength against an adversary for food, shelter or mates. Today biological fitness is not equated to physical strength, although it can play a role, but rather to reproductive fitness or reproductive success. Wallace also disagreed with Darwin's explanation of sexual selection; they had differences over human evolution; and Wallace later embraced spiritualism, whereas Darwin rejected it as unscientific.

When the joint Darwin–Wallace paper was read and published in 1858 no differences yet existed between the two authors – these conflicts only emerged some years later. More than anything at this juncture Darwin needed a respite from the tumultuous past few months. With Emma's coaxing the whole Darwin family took a much-needed holiday, travelling during early July to early August, mostly on the Isle of Wight. Darwin continued gathering his notes and producing manuscript pages – even working on his writing during a return visit to the hydropathy establishment at Moor Park in Farnham, where he would make repeat visits well into 1859 as he worked on his 'abstract'. But who would publish such a heretical work?

John Murray, the publisher of the second edition of *Darwin's Journal of Researches* in 1845, was approached and, with surprisingly few concerns, agreed. According to Carpenter's 2008 history of the seven-generation John Murray publication dynasty, John Murray III followed the usual practice of requesting comment on the manuscript from two outside reviewers. The first was the lawyer George Pollock, who noted Darwin's book was probably beyond the comprehension of most scientists but that Darwin had tackled the formidable issues of the subject. This was damning with faint praise, but the second reviewer was not even this accommodating. This was the editor of Murray's conservative *Quarterly Review*, the clergyman Whitwell Elwin, who was horrified, finding the book wild and foolish. Ever the businessman, Murray went ahead with publication, even though he later noted that the whole theory was as absurd as contemplating the successful mating of a poker and rabbit.

On 10 May 1859 Darwin sent six of the fourteen chapters of his abstract to the printers. Even after proofs of these and later manuscript pages were available soon thereafter, Darwin needed to make some obvious and not so obvious corrections, a headache for any publisher. On 1 October Darwin wrote that it had taken thirteen months and ten days to complete the proofs of his 'Abstract on the Origin of Species', but what a toll it wrought. His health was in shambles and he was racked by frequent vomiting. He straight away left for a hydropathic establishment at Wells House in Ilkley, a spa town in what is now West Yorkshire, where he stayed for the better part of two months in the hope that the water cure might once again bring some respite. During this time his health and spirits went from bad to worse and back again, though some comfort came from a family visit. On 2 November Murray sent a single copy of his book to Darwin at Ilkley, delighting Darwin with 'the appearance of my child'.[12]

Darwin was at Ilkley on 24 November when his abstract *On the Origin of Species by Means of Natural Selection, or the Preservation of Favoured Races in the Struggle for Life* was officially published. The book was priced at fifteen shillings and included fourteen chapters as well as an index, running to 502 pages. No wonder then that Murray declined Darwin's request to include the word 'abstract' in the title of such a lengthy book. The first eight chapters deal with variation and selection under both artificial and natural conditions, the struggle for existence, hybridization, instinct, and issues with his theory. The next five chapters examine the palaeontological, biogeographical, morphological and embryological information that can be brought to bear on his theory, notably multiple proofs that evolution has occurred. The last chapter is a 'recapitulation and conclusion' of the work.

There is a single fold-out figure in the book, which Darwin called an accompanying diagram. It is a hypothetical tree of life which he used to explain how his process of descent with modification worked, emphasizing what he called his principle of divergence of character. Darwin's divergence of character became an often-repeated theme in the book, more so than notions of progress through evolutionary time. This went against the emphasized ideal of progress seen both in Victorian biology and religion. In Darwin's tree diagram there are eleven ancestors labelled from A to I, K and L, shown in fourteen equally spaced time intervals identified with Roman numerals. Only two of the ancestral species show many slowly branching new species at each geological interval, whereas the other nine continue through geological time unchanged, most becoming extinct. This was not a tree to show the evolutionary history of any groups but was described extensively in the text to explain how Darwin envisioned the process of descent with modification unfolding over long stretches of geological time with stasis in most lineages and divergence in few. The predominance of stasis as an evolutionary

Six editions of *On the Origin of Species* and the first edition's cover, title page and foldout diagram.

pattern has been written about by various authors. It found its most recent iteration in the concept of punctuated equilibrium propounded in the 1970s, in which it is argued that most change occurs during speciation events. This is then followed by long periods of equilibrium or little change, similar to Darwin's argument for stasis more than 160 years ago. Although Darwin sketched a number of other similar diagrams for personal use and in correspondence to colleagues, this is his only tree-like diagram published in his lifetime.

The often-repeated story that all 1,250 copies of the book sold on the official publication date of 24 November is not correct. In addition to the copy sent to Darwin on 2 November while at Ilkley he later received twelve additional gratis author copies. In a list drawn up by Darwin he specified that ninety presentation copies were to be sent to domestic and foreign recipients, often inscribed 'From the Author' by the publisher's clerk. Murray sent out a further 41 review copies as well as five required for copyright. The remaining approximately 1,100 copies were offered by Murray's to booksellers on 22 November before publication. Mudie's, a lending library, purchased five hundred copies, assuring accessibility for the public. With so few copies left for other booksellers, the first edition was oversubscribed by 250 copies, forcing Murray to prepare another printing.

This second print run of 3,000 copies appeared on 7 January 1860. Although it is not called a second edition on the title page it is regarded as such given that the publisher and Darwin made some corrections to the original edition. The most profound change was in the last and most poetical sentence, which in the 1859 edition reads:

There is grandeur in this view of life, with its several powers, having been originally breathed into a few forms or into one; and that, whilst this planet has gone

cycling on according to the fixed law of gravity, from so
simple a beginning endless forms most beautiful and
most wonderful have been, and are being, evolved.[13]

In the 1860 second edition the phrase 'by the Creator' was added
after the word 'breathed'.[14] In 1863 Darwin confided in a letter to
Hooker that he regretted bending to public opinion by inserting
the addition – by 'the creator', he really meant an unknown cause.
'But I have long regretted that I truckled to public opinion & used
Pentateuchal term of creation, by which I really meant "appeared"
by some wholly unknown process. – It is mere rubbish thinking,
at present, of origin of life; one might as well think of origin of
matter.'[15] Why he then did not remove it in later editions remains
unclear; thus, it stayed in all subsequent editions through to the last
version upon which Darwin worked, in 1876.

As the above quote shows, the final word in all editions
of his magnum opus is 'evolved' yet he never used the word
'evolution' anywhere in the text in the first five editions of his
book. Darwin was reluctant to use this word at least in part
because of its association with the eighteenth-century concept
of preformationism that states that organisms develop from
identical miniature versions formed in the sperm or egg of their
parents. Beyond the obviously absurd logic of this idea, Darwin's
contemporary, Herbert Spencer, the originator of the phrase
'survival of the fittest', was using 'evolution' for all-encompassing
changes in the natural world. By 1868 Darwin began to bow to
popular sentiment, using the word once in his 1868 *The Variation
of Animals and Plants under Domestication* and 32 times in his 1871
The Descent of Man, and Selection in Relation to Sex to refer to his
own theory. It was only in the first appearance of the sixth edition
of *On the Origin of Species* in 1872 that Darwin used some variant of
'evolve', 'evolution' or 'evolutionist' seventeen times. The book has
never been out of print, translated into eleven languages during the

author's lifetime and at the last count into at least 35, the most of any scientific book. Today we still refer to his theory as evolution by means of natural selection.

Darwin later realized that in the first edition he was remiss in not mentioning the work of others that preceded if not actually led to his results. Accordingly, starting with the 1861 third edition published by John Murray, Darwin added what he called a 'Historical Sketch', which earlier in 1860 had appeared as shorter versions in editions published in both the United States and Germany. In 1859 Hooker had pointed out to Darwin that in an 1852 article the French natural historian Charles Victor Naudin had mentioned that species might change by processes similar to how humans cultivate domestic varieties. Darwin realized that Naudin had not suggested natural selection but he still had made the connection between changes in domesticated and wild species. Darwin expanded this to discuss those who before him had touched on the possibility of the mutability of species without reaching the more refined and complete explanation in his theory. Additionally, in correspondence between Darwin and Baden Powell of Oxford, Powell indicated that Darwin's works and results were preceded by that of others, including himself.[16] Similarly, Darwin learned that in an appendix to *Naval Timber and Arboriculture* (1831), by the Scottish merchant and forester Patrick Matthew, the author had explained the appearance of species by what Darwin now called 'natural selection'.[17] In his 'Historical Sketch' Darwin listed people to whom he attributed a belief in the 'modification of species, or [who] at least disbelieved in separate acts of creation'. By his 1866 edition he noted geologists, botanists and zoologists, as well as some who also touched on palaeontological topics.

Beyond the obvious co-discoverer of natural selection Alfred Russel Wallace, some of Darwin's other better-known contemporaries included in his sketch are Heinrich Bronn, Robert Chambers (anonymously), Henry Freke, Robert Grant, John

Herschel, Joseph Dalton Hooker, Thomas Henry Huxley, Richard Owen and Herbert Spencer. Earlier well-known persons Darwin included were Aristotle, Georges-Louis Leclerc de Buffon, Erasmus Darwin, Isidore and Étienne Geoffroy Saint-Hilaire, Jean Baptiste Julien d'Omalius d'Halloy, Johann Wolfgang von Goethe and Jean-Baptiste Lamarck. While we thank Darwin for his fastidiousness in giving credit where credit is due, he turned over every emblematic stone to acknowledge as many people as possible, deserved or not.

8

Reviews and Reactions

With the publication of his magnum opus on evolution in 1859 Charles Darwin went almost overnight from being one of the most revered, famous natural historians in the world to one of its most infamous. Until 1876, when the final version of the sixth edition appeared, many of Darwin's days were consumed in defending himself and his theory through his scientific papers, correspondence and above all his books. Darwin chose never to address critics in person, such as at scientific meetings and conferences, but he never shrank from responding to critics both in correspondence and in revisions of his text. He left public debates with critics to his staunch defenders such as Lyell, Hooker, Huxley and Wallace in England, Gray in the United States, and Ernst Haeckel in Germany. Why Darwin chose to respond to his critics in this manner remains a matter of conjecture, but a likely overriding reason was his compromised health. He certainly had not eschewed such exchanges his entire life. One need only to be reminded of his rather heated discussions with Robert FitzRoy while aboard the *Beagle*, especially when it pertained to the question of slavery, to which he was unalterably opposed. Quite simply, by the time *On the Origin of Species* appeared his health would no longer permit such in-person interactions. Although not dealing with his critics in person, Darwin certainly was not yet done telling and defending his story of evolution. After all, he had large parts of his 'big book' yet to be published. The ensuing nineteen years following publication of *On the Origin of Species* were among Darwin's most intellectually tumultuous and productive, with much of his research revealed in seven books, two of which were comprised of two volumes each. Some of these were part of what he had envisioned for his much larger work on the species question.

Within less than a month of the November publication of *On the Origin of Species*, reviews began to appear in print. Many were anonymous, as was common in nineteenth-century England. In a favourable tone, *Chambers's Journal* proclaimed that 'Mr Darwin fully expects that his views, if accepted, will revolutionise natural history.' One of the journal's editors was Robert Chambers, the then still anonymous author of the 1844 *Vestiges of Creation*, so in hindsight, one might expect a sympathetic hearing.[1] The *Saturday Review* took a more measured approach, writing that although they 'remain[ed] unconvinced', they were 'far from thinking that the fruits of his labour and research will be useless to natural science ... natural selection must henceforward be admitted as the chief mode by which the structure of organized beings is modified in a state of nature.'[2] *John Bull and Britannia* proclaimed that although Darwin's theory 'can by no means be said to be established yet ... It is surely not less a Divine act of creation, to impress a law upon nature by which she developed herself, than to create the developed forms themselves.'[3]

Many more reviews of *On the Origin of Species* ensued in the following years. In the United States, Darwin had been sharing his evolutionary theorizing with Gray since 1857, so the appearance of Darwin's book came as no surprise to Gray, who received a copy of the book from John Murray compliments of the author. In March 1860 Gray published a review in the *American Journal of Science and Arts*, now called the *American Journal of Science*. Begun in 1818, it is the longest continuously running scientific journal in the United States and at the time was a leading and influential journal in the sciences. Gray was instrumental in securing an American copyright for Darwin's book, no mean feat in the nineteenth century. Darwin held Gray in such high regard that he dedicated his book *The Different Forms of Flowers* (1877) to him, 'as a small tribute of respect and affection' – only the second of two times that Darwin dedicated a book; the first was the second edition of his *Journal of Researches*, which he dedicated to Charles Lyell in 1845.

Gray also wrote an extensive three-part review beginning in the July 1860 issue of the *Atlantic Monthly*, a magazine started in 1857 and still published today that presents broader commentaries on literary, cultural and social issues. By publishing the review in this particular magazine, Gray was able to ensure that it would reach an audience in the U.S. beyond that of scientists and academics. In 1860 the *Atlantic Monthly* carried other articles and reviews dealing with issues of far deeper concern to its American audiences – expansion of slavery westward, looming civil war, and the coming presidential elections in November, which Abraham Lincoln won with 40 per cent of the vote in a four-way race. Lincoln and Darwin by chance shared the same date and year of birth, 12 February 1809, and so both were 51 years old in 1860. Darwin had just published his magnum opus and Lincoln would soon lead a nation riven by an extremely bloody civil war.

The correspondence of Gray and Darwin reflected these dire times in America. Shortly after armed conflict began in 1861 between the United States of America and the newly proclaimed Confederate States of America, Darwin wrote to Gray that he knew of no one who did not support the North. This was certainly true of people such as himself, who were liberal Whig members of the upper middle and upper classes, as well as the more general public, but not so for more conservative elites in Britain. He opined that though the outcome may be in some doubt, if millions of lives are lost in this 'crusade against slavery' it would be 'repaid in the cause of humanity', seeing the 'greatest curse on Earth, slavery, abolished'.[4] Emma Darwin was so outraged that *The*

Times newspaper in London supported the Confederacy that she boycotted the newspaper for many years.

When Lincoln's Emancipation Proclamation was signed two years later in 1863, Darwin wrote to Gray that Lincoln had 'issued his fiat against slavery'. Although Gray wrote that 'slavery is dead, dead' Darwin remained sceptical of the outcome because of the great ravages being inflicted in the American conflict.[5] Darwin's government never recognized the Confederacy, neither signing any treaties nor exchanging ambassadors, but it granted the Confederacy 'belligerent status'. Well over 90 per cent of trade between the Confederacy and Britain had ended with a resulting catastrophic shortage of cotton. Under the wink-wink nudge-nudge version of diplomacy, Britain helped pay for blockade runners, shipping armaments and luxuries to Confederate ports with cotton and tobacco headed back home to Britain. It went even further with warships being built in Liverpool destined for the Confederate navy. War between the United States and Great Britain over trade with the South seemed a real possibility until cooler diplomatic heads prevailed.

The impending American Civil War loomed large in the British press but so too did the reactions to Darwin's shocking book. This is perhaps nowhere better seen than in the public debates that ensued on 30 June 1860 at the meeting of the British Association for the Advancement of Science, seven months after the publication of Darwin's book. It took place in Oxford's brand new 'cathedral to science', the University Museum, before the architectural details were complete and the collections fully installed. This event has resonated down the years, becoming known as the Great Debate. It has been portrayed as an exchange regarding the veracity of evolution in general, and Darwin's book in particular. In keeping with his ill health and abhorrence of the public debate of his work, Darwin was not in attendance at Oxford, preferring that others might carry the torch. The protagonists were Samuel Wilberforce

Bishop Samuel Wilberforce, an English foe of Darwin and his theory of evolution.

– the bishop of Oxford, a foe of Darwin's ideas – and the comparative anatomist Thomas Henry Huxley, who had become a staunch supporter. What actually transpired was not written down and accounts vary, but the wider consensus is that the evolutionists rightfully claimed victory while a minority view claims both sides held their own.

A prologue to the Wilberforce–Huxley exchange occurred two days earlier on 28 June at the same scientific meeting in Oxford.

Richard Owen and Huxley, both comparative anatomists, attended a lecture on sexuality in plants that supportively referenced Darwin's evolutionary ideas. What followed was an exchange that had nothing to do with plant sexuality. Owen cited his 1857 work, which argued that only humans had a portion of the brain then known as the hippocampus minor that he thought was lacking in other apes such as the gorilla – this lack was for him strong evidence against evolution. For his part, Huxley reported his own anatomical work in showing that Owen's interpretation was in error. Huxley argued that humans and other apes varied little in this region of the brain, although the brain sizes did differ. When Huxley's work on this later appeared in print, it showed his scientific interpretation as correct, casting doubt on Owen's claims as the best English comparative anatomist and more damningly his trustworthiness as a scientist. His reputation was not aided by the lampooning of this exchange as 'the great hippopotamus test' in Charles Kingsley's *The Water-babies: A Fairy Tale for a Land Baby,* first serialized in *Macmillan's Magazine* in 1862–3 and then published as a book later in 1863. Although the book obliquely supported and popularized Darwin's work on evolution, Kingsley's satire often provided even-handed skewering. Owen and Huxley were shown as an amalgamated character named Professor Ptthmllnsprts (Put-them-all-in-spirits) – a name that obviously satirized their propensity for using preserved specimens in public lectures.[6]

The hippocampus minor brouhaha primed the two sides for the Wilberforce–Huxley exchange that followed on 30 June. It was not a formal debate but rather a heated exchange during a discussion that followed a rather dry talk by the British-born American philosopher and scientist John William Draper. Draper's talk focused on European intellectual development in light of Darwin's findings, and the session and following discussion were chaired by Darwin's Cambridge mentor John Stevens Henslow. The overflow audience was not there for Draper but for the anticipated fireworks from the anti-Darwinian remarks by Wilberforce, who was almost certainly coached by Owen. The audience was not disappointed, but the bloviating Wilberforce made, by most accounts, a tactical error in supposedly asking Huxley if it was through his grandfather or his grandmother that he claimed his descent from a monkey. Huxley purportedly whispered to the man sitting next to him, Sir Benjamin Brodie, that the Lord has delivered Wilberforce unto his hands. Huxley then replied to the audience to the effect that if asked whether he would rather have a miserable ape for a grandfather or a man highly endowed by nature and possessing great influence who employed these faculties for the mere purpose of introducing ridicule into a grave scientific discussion, he unhesitatingly affirmed his preferences for the ape. Little else of what Huxley said was recalled by the audience, but this remark was considered at least by the Darwin supporters as a triumph, whether or not it was what Huxley actually said.

Following Huxley's remarks, a Bible-waving, some say slightly unhinged, man in the audience denounced Darwin's blasphemy. This was Robert FitzRoy, now a rear admiral, who reportedly felt guilty for his decision all those years ago to have brought Darwin on the voyage of the *Beagle*. FitzRoy's career and finances had been star-crossed, from the Admiralty's disapproval of his purchase of the *Adventure* during the second voyage of the *Beagle* to his ill-fated governorship of New Zealand. By the time of the debate in Oxford in 1860 FitzRoy had been running the office that dealt with weather forecasting, which was particularly important for saving lives in maritime pursuits. He was ahead of his time in this regard, but even here he faced stiff opposition from some members of the Admiralty. All of this was taking its toll, such that in 1865 FitzRoy took his life by slitting his throat with a razor – the same manner of death as his uncle, Robert Stewart, Viscount Castlereagh, who committed suicide in 1822.

The final remarks at the debate were by Darwin's great friend and colleague J. D. Hooker, who solidified support for the Darwinist position among members of the audience. The whole affair received only passing notice in the press, but over the years became a seminal turning point in the acceptance of evolution if not Darwin and Wallace's concept of natural selection. Within months of the Oxford exchange two notably negative reviews of Darwin appeared and, although presented anonymously, it was well-known that one, in the *Quarterly Review*, was authored by Wilberforce and the other, in the *Edinburgh Review*, by Owen.[7] Wilberforce's review, although glossed with a veneer of science, devolves into a mostly religious argument. It begins in praise of Darwin for his style of presentation and the considerable efforts he expended, but for Wilberforce it is unequivocal that each species has an unchanging existence in nature – each species is endowed with its distinct 'attributes and organization' at the time of its creation. He finishes by mocking the idea of finding changes in species, equating them to the likelihood of finding mythical beasts such as centaurs, hippogriffs (a legendary animal with the head and wings of an eagle and the rear body of a horse) and men known as blemmyes, who have no head but a face in their chest.

Owen's review, in addition to being one of the most negative, was among the most supercilious. He first damned Darwin with faint praise, then proceeded to quote in full the first sentence of Darwin's book only to follow this with the snide comment that nothing in the book shed light on the origin of any species, including humans. Never mind that Darwin had yet to write anything about human origins. After prattling on about indigenous South Americans, sponges and plants, Owen concluded that the book offered no evidence that would shed light on the origin of species. One instance that seemed to sting was Owen's rebuke regarding Darwin's story of the North American black bear, which was seen swimming for hours with its mouth open, whale-like, to catch insects.[8] He openly imagined that over time, given an ample supply of insects and no other competitors, natural selection would make these bears more and more aquatic, eventually producing a whale. Although an interesting thought experiment, it provided plenty of ammunition for his adversaries to ridicule, and Owen did both in print and in correspondence. Lyell suggested that Darwin lose the example in the second edition. From the second edition onwards, Darwin kept the part about the bear but only the description of its insect-catching behaviour mimicking a whale's, no longer writing that over time it could evolve into a whale.

Wilberforce's views held little sway in the scientific community, and Owen's otherwise well-earned fame as an anatomist was tarnished by his ego and duplicity; he was far from an honest broker in evaluating Darwin's book. He is often portrayed as an anti-evolutionist, but in fact he accepted evolution; his argument was that it was far more complicated than Darwin's theory claimed. Because Owen never really committed himself to an alternate theory of how evolution transpired, all we are left with is a rather befuddled idea: that embryological similarities somehow lead back to an archetype which originated in the mind of God. He was jealous of Darwin's success. He had worked well with Darwin in the 1830s producing the fine contribution on the fossil mammals in the *Zoology*, but this relationship had soured.

Richard Owen appeared on a rather curious list of those whom Darwin called 'immutabilists' in his chapter dealing with the imperfection of the geological record.[9] Among the palaeontological immutabilists were the anatomist Georges Cuvier, who had died in 1832; Owen was second; third was the Swiss-American Louis Agassiz; next was the Frenchman Joachim Barrande, then the Swiss scientist François Jules Pictet de la Rive, and Scotsman Hugh Falconer and English naturalist Edward Forbes rounded out the names. The geological immutabilists were Adam Sedgwick, Roderick Impey Murchison and Charles Lyell. Lyell received the dubious honour of being a doubter rather than an out-and-out immutabilist. Even though Lyell was always at least somewhat doubtful of Darwin's 'natural selection', he remained a loyal friend and a staunch supporter. Why Darwin bothered to produce such a list remains somewhat opaque, but at the very least it registered Darwin's enormous concern with the geological and palaeontological records in support of evolution. Over the subsequent five editions Darwin added a few other 'immutabilists' but removed only one person from the list – Owen.

In a letter to Darwin in November 1859, after receiving a copy of Darwin's book, Owen wrote that in fact he was open to some sort of species mutability. Because of Owen's objection to being placed on the list of 'immutabilists' Darwin removed his name in later editions. Shortly after reading Owen's letter, Darwin wrote to Lyell that the anatomist feigned a 'garb of civility' but in the end he thought Owen was in general agreement with his theory.[10] He was sorely mistaken, for a few months later in early 1860 Owen's savage criticism of Darwin and his theory appeared in the *Edinburgh Review*. Owen's true nature and sentiments had been revealed. Why Darwin never returned him to the list of 'immutabilists' is unknown.

Owen's and Wilberforce's objections to Darwin's theory were among many such critiques that could not point to a specific problem with the theory. They simply found fault with the whole idea outright because it often seemed to displace God as the creator of the universe and its creatures therein. In Owen's case, however, jealousy that he had not thought of the idea first clearly played a role. Beyond these sorts of general dismissals were three broader concerns that had been raised by more penetrating critics, and these were the ones to vex Darwin for the rest of his life. The first critique pertained to issues regarding the age of Earth and the quality of the fossil record. The second asked how natural selection could possibly work given what was then known about inheritance.

Third, critics asked how complex organs such as eyes or wings could evolve through the gradual process of natural selection. Darwin satisfactorily answered this last objection, but the solutions to the first two were answered only some twenty years after Darwin's death thanks to advances in scientific knowledge.

The first question would not be answered until well into the twentieth century, when geochronological dating techniques made use of radioactive isotopes and palaeomagnetism to provide us with knowledge of great expanses of geological time and an accurate method to measure the age of Earth to at least 4.5 billion years. To be clear, everyone, not just Darwin, struggled with the problem of dating fossils and the rocks they contained. In his eagerness, Darwin stumbled badly in addressing this issue as he had in his geological misinterpretation of the Parallel Roads of Glen Roy some twenty years earlier.

Although the aforementioned *Saturday Review* had been positive in some of its comments on Darwin's theory it had also included a lengthy critique of how Darwin attempted to determine the passage of geological time. In order to make the case that Earth was very old, Darwin made an imprudent estimate that the Weald in southeast England had taken 300 million years to be sculpted by erosion.[11] Thus, Darwin argued, the Earth must be considerably older. The Weald includes a central low area bounded north and south by escarpments known as the North and South Downs. The well-known White Cliffs of Dover form part of these downs on the south, facing the English Channel. The anonymous *Saturday Review* critic, who may have been the Oxford geologist John Phillips, pounced. The reviewer argued, and most agreed, that Darwin's estimate of time for erosion of the Weald was vastly exaggerated. The actual time it took to erode the Weald was far less than that calculated by Darwin. We know today that some of its clay deposits were not even deposited until 130 million years ago. Taking heed of his critics, Darwin removed the Weald calculation from the 1861 third edition as well as all later editions. He felt that he needed an immensely ancient Earth for the very slow processes of natural selection to act upon organisms in order to bring about evolutionary change, but the erosion of the Weald could not provide this. Time, notably of a very old Earth, was of the essence, but a more accurate estimate eluded not just Darwin but all who tried to guess it until well into the twentieth century.

The eighteenth-century Scottish geologist James Hutton had argued that Earth had no vestige of a beginning nor prospect of an end, thus making it ageless. Charles Lyell championed Hutton's ideas. Whereas most did not subscribe to the notion of an ageless Earth advocated by Hutton and Lyell, the idea that Earth was aeons old slowly gained acceptance even if it was not yet provable and it became the proverbial linch-pin of Darwin's evolution by natural selection. Soon criticism even harsher than that resulting from the Weald erosion debacle emerged espousing an even more damning dismissal for an ancient Earth. The critic was not a geologist but the Belfast-born physicist William Thomson, awarded his title Lord Kelvin for his scientific achievements and his efforts at preventing Irish home rule.

Thomson's criticism came only three years after Darwin's 1859 publication of *On the Origin of Species* and a year after the third edition appeared in 1861. In his 1862 article Thomson argued that the Sun 'has not illuminated the earth for 100,000,000 years, and almost certainly that it has not done so for 500,000,000 years', thus Earth could not be older than this figure.[12] A truer aim of Thomson was to show geologists in general and Lyell in particular, with Darwin thrown in for good measure, the error of their ways. Thomson took direct aim at Darwin's estimate of 300 million years for the denudation of the Weald, never mind that Darwin had dropped this example in his third edition of 1861 a year before Thomson's article was published. In the fourth edition of *On the Origin of Species* in 1866, Darwin still did not respond to Thomson's already well-circulated ideas on the brevity of Earth's history. By the fifth edition in 1869, Darwin finally felt compelled to respond. It seemed a half-hearted attempt to compromise by discussing the difficulty of contemplating great expanses of time. Deep time would remain a major issue for everyone.

In one of those twists of fate, Darwin's second oldest son and fifth child George acted as a sometime mediator between Thomson and his father over the age of Earth. Although George had studied law at the University of Cambridge and had even been admitted to the bar, he returned to science and made a considerable name for himself in geophysics and astronomy. It was as a young man that he worked with Thomson on tides and Earth's composition. He would go on to have a distinguished career as a Cambridge professor of astronomy, marrying in 1884 the American Martha du Puy, with whom he had five children. Darwin never met these grandchildren, dying three years before the birth of the oldest, Gwen Raverat. George never convinced his father of Thomson's position, but did suggest that the timescale might be shorter than his father thought was needed for natural selection to operate.

There was also the related problem of the poor quality of the fossil record, but unlike the conundrum of estimating geological time the fossil record was becoming better with each passing year, offering a light at the end of this particularly problematic tunnel. Curiously, in one instance Darwin essentially failed to pounce upon what was then and still is today an excellent example of a fossil species possessing characteristics which bridge two major groups. The fossil is *Archaeopteryx*, which Darwin misspelled as *Archeopteryx*, and the two groups are reptiles and birds. Today it is widely accepted that birds are united with theropod dinosaurs within Reptilia, but this was not brought to light until the 1960s, yet the prescient T. H. Huxley made this suggestion, with little support, in 1868.

Archaeopteryx was first described in 1861 based on a single feather found in the Solnhofen Limestone of southern Germany dating to some 150 million years ago in the Late Jurassic Period. A nearly complete specimen, which was at first erroneously thought to lack all traces of the skull, was unearthed and then sold to the British Museum for £700, equivalent to £86,000 today. At least eleven further specimens have been assigned to *Archaeopteryx*. Richard Owen described the London specimen with much fanfare in 1863.[13] The specimen shows many transitional characteristics between non-bird dinosaurs and birds but given his lack of public support for evolutionary theories, Owen certainly would not have called attention to its transitional nature, only its great age. By the fourth edition of *On the Origin of Species* in 1866 Charles Darwin mentioned *Archaeopteryx*. Surprisingly, Darwin also did not emphasize its transitional nature; rather, he used it as an example of a sudden appearance of a group in the fossil record much earlier than thought, which in the case of birds extended their range from the Eocene back to the Late Jurassic. Others, such as the German palaeontologist Friedrich Rolle, were more impassioned about what the transitional nature of *Archaeopteryx* revealed concerning Darwin's theory. In a postscript to his 1867 book *Der Archaeopteryx oder Urvogel der Jura-Zeit* (The *Archaeopteryx* or Primeval Bird of the Jurassic Period) Rolle remarked that *Archaeopteryx* bridges the evolutionary gap that Darwin's theory predicted. He indicated that its feathers and feet were like those of living birds, whereas the tail resembled that of a lizard. For whatever reason Darwin never emphasized this transitional nature.

Whereas Darwin did not use *Archaeopteryx* to all its potential in support of his theory, in the same fourth edition in 1866 he lauded the discovery of *Eozoön,* identified as a microscopic 'dawn animal of Canada' thought to be a gigantic single-celled planktonic animal known as foraminiferans that lives in the sea. It was described at the 1864 meeting of the British Association for the Advancement of Science.[14] The sobriquet 'dawn animal of Canada' was earned because it was discovered in what were then some of the oldest-known rocks on Earth, what we today identify as Precambrian in age, in Quebec. Darwin touted it as 'the great discovery of the Eozoon . . . a remarkable fossil, it is impossible to feel any doubt regarding its organic nature'; he spoke of its extraordinarily ancient age, being something far older than any other fossil discovered to date.[15] In the ensuing years doubts were raised about the organic nature of *Eozoön,* such that by the time the sixth edition first appeared in 1872, Darwin only commented that 'the existence of the Eozoon in the Laurentian formation of Canada is generally admitted.'[16] By the end of the nineteenth century the ancient age of the deposits was confirmed but *Eozoön* was shown to be a pseudofossil in metamorphic rocks. Desperately trying to show the ancient age of Earth, Darwin, like others, quickly accepted the validity of *Eozoön* yet failed to take advantage of *Archaeopteryx,* which would have been a substantial boost to his arguments for transitional forms.

The second and also seemingly insurmountable problem for the theory was how characteristics in one generation were passed from one generation to the next. Darwin was working on this problem in his 'big book' and thought he had an answer; this would not appear for a number of years and thus he provided few particulars in the first edition of *On the Origin of Species* in 1859. In the nineteenth century it was believed that characteristics of parents were blended in their offspring. This was not an unreasonable assertion as offspring generally appeared to have a combination of characteristics from both parents, although unexplained appearances of characters or so-called 'sports' could arise that differed from either parent (though these were perhaps similar to features of a grandparent). Darwin's natural selection might favour the survival and reproductive success of the individual with this unique new feature or sport but there was a problem, as Edinburgh professor Fleeming Jenkin so clearly articulated in his rather belated 1867 appraisal in the *North British Review* of the 1859 first edition of *On the Origin of Species*.[17] Jenkin noted that even if sports should arise, they eventually would be swamped by blending inheritance, which means the characters would be an average of those of the parents, and after just a few generations such peculiarities would be obliterated. Because of blending inheritance, natural selection could not work over the long haul of geological time. As it turned out, some of Jenkin's mathematical calculations were in error, but his general argument of the swamping effect held and was damning for Darwin's blending inheritance.

Darwin was correct about how natural selection operated but what he could not know was that it required particulate rather than blending inheritance. In this way characters would be passed on as discrete bits of information that natural selection could act upon in the individual, rather than becoming swamped and disappearing as Jenkin had argued. In fact, particulate inheritance had been reported in 1866, just two years before Jenkin's review, by Gregor Mendel, but most of the scientific community including Darwin and Jenkin had heard nothing of Mendel's studies.[18] An urban legend continues to circulate that Darwin received one of the forty reprints of Mendel's paper, but nothing in Darwin's archives exists to support such a claim. Even if Darwin had known of Mendel's work, he probably would not have connected it to his own work. Another story that does not rise to the level of an urban legend asks why Mendel did not visit Darwin when he attended the 1862 Industrial Exhibition in London. After all, the village of Downe was only around 30 kilometres (less than 20 miles) away. First, it probably never occurred to Mendel to attempt to visit to such a well-known scientist as Darwin with whom he had little in common. Second, at this time the Darwin family were attending to their son Leonard, who was very ill with scarlet fever, and they were not entertaining guests. By the early 1900s, almost twenty years after Darwin's death, Mendel's work was rediscovered independently by several botanists, and Mendel's particulate inheritance was proven to be correct. Further, it was not until the 1930s that population geneticists and naturalists put Darwin's natural selection together with Mendel's particulate inheritance to show that in combination these were some of the major driving forces of evolution.

During Darwin's lifetime, in later editions of *On the Origin of Species* he did satisfactorily answer the third objection to his theory: how complex organs such as eyes or wings evolved through the gradual process of natural selection. From the first edition Darwin had argued that evolutionary processes must be gradual; he used the well-known Latin phrase *natura non facit saltum* (nature does not make jumps) some eight times in his book. The person who brought the issue of complex organs to a head was St George Jackson Mivart. Mivart was a conflicted person who struggled with problems both self-inflicted and imposed upon him by circumstance. Although raised as an evangelical Christian, as a young man he converted to Roman Catholicism. This immediately precluded him from furthering his education at such institutions as Oxford and Cambridge, which were staunchly Church of England. Although Mivart qualified for the bar in 1851, he turned his interests to the biological sciences. These interests were stimulated by his friend T. H. Huxley, who imbued him with the new ideas advocated in Darwin's book on evolution. Mivart was at first a true acolyte, even publishing papers in the 1860s in which he presented parts of the primate skeleton as they applied to evolution of the group, producing some of the earliest evolutionary trees inspired by Darwin's work.[19] The application of Darwin's ideas to phylogenetic work or how species are related was innovative and Mivart, like other young scientists, leapt at the prospect of unravelling how species were related rather than simply producing dry species descriptions.

Soon, however, Mivart turned against Darwin's ideas, in part because of his own Catholicism, which rejected evolution, and in part because of the strident anti-Catholicism of notable people like Huxley, whom Mivart had at first admired and considered a mentor. Mivart struck at Darwin both professionally and personally. On the professional side, Mivart published *On the Genesis of Species* in 1871 in an attempt to replace Darwin's natural selection with some sort of 'internal force or tendency'.[20] If he thought such teleological argumentation would be more in keeping with his Catholic faith, he was mistaken. The Catholic Church would have none of it, nor would the Church condone his lenient views on the nature of Hell, thus making him a pariah in both Catholic and evolutionary circles. Nevertheless, Darwin took seriously Mivart's arguments about how natural selection over long stretches of time could not produce complex organs such as eyes, wings or lungs. How, then, could half an organ possibly function? Beginning in the 1872 sixth edition, in the case of the eye, Darwin showed that among living animals one could find any number of stages going from simple light-sensitive organs through to complex structures complete with lenses. Using these modern examples, he showed that natural selection could in fact produce a complex organ through multiple small steps with each species well adapted to its environment. In this instance Darwin soundly addressed his critics, if not completely silenced them.[21]

Darwin was certainly not above striking back at his detractors and held Mivart in this class of contempt. Mivart wrote a quite inimical review of *Descent of Man* in the *Quarterly Review* that Darwin regarded as 'grossly unfair' as Mivart misquoted Darwin and took passages out of context.[22] As a form of retribution, Darwin arranged and paid for the republication in England of a scathing review of Mivart's *Genesis of Species* that had first been published in the United States by Darwin supporter and correspondent Chauncey Wright.

It was, however, Mivart's personal attack of Darwin's son George that truly vexed Darwin and his followers. George had published an article in 1873 in which he advocated easing strictures on divorce in cases of abuse, cruelty and mental disorders. Mivart was apoplectic, misrepresenting George's position as advocating sexual criminality and licentiousness. Darwin and colleagues, notably Mivart's former friend Huxley, turned on him with a vengeance, largely ostracizing him from major scientific circles.

George had not just written on easing strictures on divorce. In 1870 he began studying the health of children from first-cousin marriages. This was in part through the urging of his father, who had always been worried about his and Emma's union as first cousins, especially as they had lost three of their ten children. At that time in England there was considerable debate as to whether consanguineous marriages such as theirs were detrimental to the health of the offspring. Darwin also had additional knowledge that could have worried him. He was commencing studies on the effects of cross- and self-fertilization in plants and this provided him with information on the likely effects of inbreeding. George examined marriages between close relatives in asylums, comparing them to the prevalence of this practice among the general population. He published his study in 1875 and with some relief to his father found that supposed ills of marriages between first cousins were often greatly exaggerated and were not significant when conditions of life were favourable.

We know that these criticisms of Darwin and members of his family took their toll. In a letter to Wallace in 1871, about the time that Mivart's disparaging book appeared, Darwin expressed considerable angst and claimed to be suffering from illness caused by what he considered overwhelming and protracted criticisms of his work. He remarked that at present he felt sick of everything. Unless he could otherwise occupy his time and forget his daily miseries, he would never publish another word. He then admitted in the same letter that he might cheer up, as he had just recovered from one of his debilitating attacks. But his angst seemed to never cease, for in this correpondence, Darwin remarked on the great sting he felt from Thomson's arguments for a much-shortened age for Earth history, remarking that it stalked him like 'an odious spectre'.[23]

Darwin persevered; in the intervening years between 1859 and 1876 across six reworked editions of *On the Origin of Species*, Darwin substantially subtracted such problematic issues as the Weald erosion and added other sections and chapters in response to his various critics, in the end adding one new chapter and more than 40,000 words. Like no person before, he had made acceptance of evolution a reality in the minds of the majority of scientists and for a large swathe of the general population. His greatest frustration was that his treasured evolutionary mechanism, natural selection, instead of becoming more and more widely accepted as time wore on gradually receded into the background. From its introduction to well into the twentieth century, natural selection led a chequered existence.

Certainly, his critics continued their harangues about the efficacy of natural selection but even his strongest supporters and colleagues such as Gray, Hooker, Lyell and Huxley had their doubts. Even Darwin's co-discoverer Wallace began to question the importance, nature and universality of natural selection when applied to humans. Tempered by these doubts is the fact that all these individuals wholeheartedly supported Darwin's endeavours even while they had qualms about particulars. This is true of any such groundbreaking strides in science.

Although one of Darwin's letters to Gray was included in the 1858 Darwin–Wallace paper announcing their theory to the world, Gray still had reservations. While being a friend, colleague and always a staunch supporter of Darwin, Gray and Charles held fundamentally different views about God's role in creation. Gray saw God's hand as the ultimate designer controlling evolution by means of natural selection, whereas Darwin saw no need of God in the process – a textbook example of agreeing to disagree when required among friends. Some version of this theistic evolution is still extant today for people needing to reconcile evolution with their belief in God.

Next, Hooker, one of Darwin's closest friends and long-time supporters, began to emphasize the importance of variation among individuals rather than natural selection acting upon given species of plant or animal. Whereas Darwin saw variation as the important raw material upon which natural selection acted, Hooker came to believe that variation in and of itself was a driver of evolution, even calling natural selection his variation theory.

Darwin's oldest friend in this circle, Lyell, while prodding Darwin to publish his ideas, always remained reticent regarding the veracity of natural selection, partly on religious grounds and partly for scientific reasons. Darwin had long been trying to change the mind of his old master about the veracity of natural selection. Darwin greatly anticipated the publication of Lyell's *Geological Evidences of the Antiquity of Man* in 1863 as he hoped that it would finally and firmly place the former mentor in Darwin's camp. This was not to be, as Lyell remained lukewarm in his acceptance of natural selection for he still had to allow for God's hand in the process. The closest that Lyell came to finding a near final acceptance of natural selection was in the tenth edition of his famous *Principles of Geology*, published 1866–8.

Darwin's most vocal and pugnacious supporter, as witnessed by his intellectual tussle with Wilberforce, was Huxley. His first reaction to natural selection was to proclaim that it was stupid of him not to have thought of the idea himself. Huxley coined the word 'agnostic' in 1869, which is a term usually applied theologically as to whether one can know if God does or does not exist. Huxley, however, meant it much more broadly. For him, an agnostic is one who goes as far as one might with the evidence at hand but does not make pronouncements beyond what is demonstrable. For him natural selection was a good start for understanding how evolution worked but it remained only one of several hypotheses.

What of Wallace, Darwin's co-discoverer of natural selection? Although obviously supporting the fruits of their separate efforts, Wallace expressed his concern that the use of the word 'selection' implied that nature somehow was selecting, as a farmer might select a favoured trait for breeding. Wallace preferred Herbert Spencer's phrase 'survival of the fittest',[24] which Darwin mistakenly accepted as an equally valid definer of the mechanism. Over time a rift in the acceptance of the universality of 'natural selection' began to separate the co-discoverers. Whereas Darwin maintained that it applied to animals and humans alike, Wallace began to argue that it could not account for many human manifestations, notably the appearance of consciousness. Darwin despaired when he contemplated Wallace's teleological arguments for some preordained purpose and directionality to evolution, notably of humans.

During this time Wallace also began to embrace spiritualism and believed that humans could contact the spirits of the dead. Wallace was not alone in this conviction among English intelligentsia, as others such as Charles Dickens and Arthur Conan Doyle also succumbed to this repeatedly debunked practice. One might argue that Darwin too was taken in by such charlatans because he partook of such questionable cures as Dr Gully's 'water cure', yet Darwin's son Francis claimed that his father was repelled by Gully's belief in homeopathy and spiritualism. The difference in the positions that Darwin and Wallace held is manifest in the court case for fraud against the American spiritualist Henry Slade in London in October 1876. It was found that Slade's board, upon which the alleged spirit was intended to write, already had writing on it before the seance began. Wallace testified on Slade's behalf and contributed £10 for his defence; Darwin donated £10 to aid in his prosecution.

Finally, we come to the reaction of Darwin's Cambridge mentor John Stevens Henslow, who more than anyone transformed Darwin from a dilettante of natural history into a bona fide scientific natural historian. Henslow was sent a copy of Darwin's book by the publisher but at least publicly his response was at first muted until early 1861, after which time his name had been included in a group of Darwin supporters composed of Huxley, Hooker and Lyell in a review of Darwin by Henry Fawcett. In his retort Henslow wrote that although Darwin's conclusions were 'surely a stumble in the right direction' and that he had 'the greatest respect for [his] friend's opinions' he could not 'assent to his speculations without seeing stronger proofs that he has yet produced'.[25]

In the time leading up to and for several years following the publication of his scientific and societal bombshell, Darwin's health wavered. His correspondence, notably letters he received, increased considerably and fortunately for us he began retaining rather than discarding many of them. His public appearances by contrast decreased, in part because he found any public spectacle regarding his work on evolution extremely disconcerting. He now commenced what one might call two tracks in his research and publication – one dealt with organizing and updating the parts from his 'big book' to support his already published 'abstract' on evolution by means of natural selection and the second was his extensive foray into botanical topics. At first glance they might seem diverging subject areas, yet all the work was in the service of proving the universality of his evolutionary ideas.

9

Bringing the 'Big Book' to Fruition

In 1862, at one of his increasingly scarce participations at scientific meetings, Darwin gave a talk at the Linnean Society in London. In the talk he was able to demonstrate that what had mistakenly been thought to be three different genera of orchids were in fact the male, female and hermaphroditic forms of a single species of the genus *Catasetum*.[1] This talk was an extract and advertisement for his first book on a botanical topic. The book was a study of orchids, or more precisely their fertilization. Its typically long Victorian title was *On the Various Contrivances by Which British and Foreign Orchids are Fertilised by Insects*, published again by John Murray, and it appeared a month after his talk.

Darwin would also soon sport a new physical look. That same spring Emma suggested that Charles grow a beard to deal with his severe facial eczema, not as has sometimes been reported to intentionally disguise himself. It eventually grew into the long, full beard recognized by most people today as representative of the great man. He had been scarce enough at many scientific gatherings that when he attended a soirée of the Royal Society in London in 1866 many did not recognize him because of the massive beard he now wore. The legend that he grew it as a disguise nonetheless worked for this purpose admirably well. His great friend J. D. Hooker remarked in a letter to Darwin soon after the Royal Society gathering that Darwin's face was a 'startling apparition . . . which I dreamed of 2 nights running'.[2]

The response to his orchid book compared to *On the Origin of Species* three years earlier was dramatic, although the orchid book did not at first sell very well. Controversy sells books, and this new one was not controversial, but interest grew. After all it was about one of the then great English passions – orchids. While some readers found the beauty inherent in orchids and Darwin's treatment of them a testament to God's glory, these same readers missed the new evidence the work provided for the efficacy of Darwin's natural selection. Uncharacteristically and uniquely for a Murray book published during Darwin's lifetime, the first edition was bound in a plum-coloured cloth with a gilt orchid on the front cover. For later editions and for all of Darwin's other books Murray chose a dark forest green colour. Most botanists praised the book and his dear American botanist friend Asa Gray wrote to him that if his orchid book 'had appeared before the "Origin," the author would have been canonised rather than anathematised by the natural theologians'.[3]

In this volume Darwin provided one of the most intriguing and precise predications in the annals of biology. The length of the nectar-secreting structure in orchids known as the nectary correlates rather well to the length of the proboscis of the pollinating insects. Darwin measured the nectary of a particular Malagasy orchid which amazingly was 29 centimetres (11½ in.) in length. In seeing the importance of cooperation between insects and plants as imparted by natural selection, Darwin realized that there must be an undiscovered insect with a proboscis the same length as this nectary. In his review of the book, George Campbell, 8th Duke of Argyll, mistook this prediction of correlation of structures for some sort of implied purpose of a creator.[4] In 1903 a moth was discovered in Madagascar with the requisitely long proboscis and many years later it was photographed in the act of feeding on and pollinating the orchid, a process of co-adaptation through natural selection, not divine purpose. Evolution can

Orchid design on the cover of *Fertilisations of Orchids* and a speculative 1867 illustration of a then unknown moth pollinating the Malagasy orchid *Angraecum sesquipedale*.

on some occasions be a predictive science and in this exquisite instance the proof came long after the death of Darwin.

In cases of co-adaptation, when evolutionary changes have played back and forth through time to produce two or more species often tightly coordinated in their anatomy, function and behaviour, the actions of natural selection are quite obvious and ubiquitous. Darwin realized the important correlation between natural selection and the adaptations and co-adaptations it produced, increasing the chances of an individual's survival which in turn increased the chances of the species's survival. Darwin thought the concept of adaptation so central to his theory that he used some form of the word more than one hundred times in different forms in the first edition of *On the Origin of Species* and more than 150 times by the publication of the sixth edition. He even used some variation of the word 'adaptation' 64 times in his orchid book. Darwin recognized that when related species descend from a common ancestor, each species, during the process of modification, becomes adapted to the conditions of life of its own region, arguing that new species supplant and exterminate their original parent and all the transitional varieties between past and present states. We now do not subscribe to his prerequisite of a descendant species extirpating its parent species, but Darwin was heading in the right direction. Extinctions occur through competition, usually with members of the same or a related species or from environmental exigencies both fast and slow.

We now recognize as a direct outgrowth of his emphasis on adaptation what we call an adaptive radiation. Darwin did not use this phrase but recognized the process that occurs when an ancestral species rapidly evolves into a variety of new species with varying degrees of morphological and behavioural differences. This may occur when an environmental setting, such as the Galápagos archipelago, presents new opportunities or challenges for an ancestral species that has arrived there from a different environment. An example of this is finches (now tanagers): an ancestral species reached the Galápagos Islands a few million years ago and radiated into as many as thirteen species, each showing a variety of environmental adaptations.

After his first not-so-timid foray into botany Darwin now turned full force to bringing much of his 'big book' to fruition in the form of three works in a total of five volumes appearing in the short interval of only four years. *The Variation of Animals and Plants under Domestication* came first, in 1868, in two volumes. In this Darwin dealt with the question of variations found in domesticated plants and animals, and he introduced his theory of inheritance. In 1865 he had written to Huxley asking him to read a manuscript on his theory of inheritance, which he called Pangenesis. Huxley's response was not very promising, as he suggested that Darwin's ideas harked back to the ideas of early nineteenth-century French evolutionists. Although Huxley could not provide much support for Darwin's ideas, he nonetheless responded facetiously, 'Somebody rummaging among your papers half a century hence will find Pangenesis & say "See this wonderful anticipation of our modern Theories – and that stupid ass, Huxley, prevented his publishing them".'[5] Darwin was justifiably concerned that this ponderous work would not be widely read or appreciated. He sent copies to colleagues in England, notably his good friend and confidant Hooker, as well as to Gray in the U.S. and the German naturalist Fritz Müller – all were accompanied by somewhat self-deprecating letters. He wanted to champion his pet theory of inheritance, but he knew it would be the proverbial hard sell among naturalists. He did at first find support among scientists such as the Dutch botanist Hugo de Vries and the German evolutionary biologist August Weismann.

Darwin theorized that organs in an animal produced minuscule particles, which he named gemmules. These would circulate in the animal and eventually find their way to the reproductive system. These gemmules could lie dormant over several generations, cause blended inheritance of traits or be affected by the environment in a Lamarckian fashion. During reproduction, gemmules of the parents mingled, forming requisite organs in individuals of the next generation. At first supporters of Darwin's ideas, such as the scientists de Vries and Weismann in the late nineteenth century, realized the impossibilities of this sort of blending, especially after the rediscovery of Mendel's experiments showing that variations were inherited in discrete or particulate packages of information. In various correspondences Darwin came close to toying with what we acknowledge as particulate or discrete inheritance of characters, but these efforts came to naught and were decidedly overshadowed by his Pangenesis.[6] The only lasting piece of Darwin's theory was the name 'pangene', which was shortened to 'gene', a term still used today.

In the summer of 1868, following on the heels of the publication of *Variation under Domestication* at the beginning of the year, the

Darwin family rented a small house for two months in Freshwater on the Isle of Wight. The home was owned by Julia Margaret Cameron, who became famous for photographing Victorian notables. She also was known for her photographs of re-enactments of mythological, biblical and literary characters. Her technique of soft-focus close-ups received both praise and criticism. Although she produced some nine hundred photographs, her career spanned only twelve years. While the Darwins were on the Isle of Wight, Cameron took well-known and now highly valued photographs of Charles, as well as of his brother Ras and Charles's son Horace. She would not photograph Emma Darwin, contending that a woman should not be photographed between the ages of eighteen and seventy. Emma noted that on one visit to Cameron's home the Darwins and J. D. Hooker met the Poet Laureate Alfred, Lord Tennyson, who had purchased a home on the Isle of Wight. On a separate occasion that summer Darwin also made a visit to Tennyson at his home Farringford House. Emily Sellwood, Tennyson's wife, noted that her husband said to Darwin that his theory was not against Christianity, to which Darwin replied that certainly it was not. Although a revered poet, reports by Henrietta (Darwin) Litchfield suggest that Tennyson did not charm or interest the Darwins.[7]

By contrast, the family did hold the renowned English novelist George Eliot, the pen name of Mary Ann or Marian Evans, in great esteem. In the evenings at Down House her novels and those of other popular writers would be read aloud by the family. In his various correspondences Charles indicated the Darwin family had read and especially liked Eliot's *Adam Bede* (1859), *The Mill on the Floss* (1860), *Silas Marner* (1861) and probably others as well. In 1868 Darwin met her and George Henry Lewes at their home in London. Eliot and Lewes were not married, a rather scandalous arrangement in Victorian England. In 1873 the Darwins rented a house at Portland Place, London, for parts of the months of March and April. This would afford the opportunity for more of the family to visit Eliot and Lewes. Darwin sent Eliot a rather fawning letter asking whether Emma, their oldest daughter Henrietta (now married to Richard Buckley Litchfield) and he might call upon her and Lewes some Sunday evening.[8] Eliot agreed and the Darwins and Litchfields visited the pair at their home. The living arrangements of Eliot and Lewes appear to have been of little concern to the rather broadminded Darwins. Charles was also favourably disposed towards Lewes because of his support for Darwin's Pangenesis, his much-maligned theorizing on inheritance. Lewes even wrote a favourable anonymous review of *Variation under Domestication* in the *Pall Mall Gazette* that Darwin greatly enjoyed.[9] Since its appearance in 1868, the two-volume work had found little traction among those who most mattered to Darwin – other scientists.

Darwin had promised to shed light on human evolution in his 1859 *On the Origin of Species*, but it took him twelve years to bring this to fruition in the next part of his 'big book'. Because this topic could prove to be especially controversial, he entrusted much of the editing of this new manuscript to his oldest surviving daughter Henrietta 'Etty'. He especially asked her to serve as a sentinel against his use of words or phrases that could be misconstrued or otherwise damaging. She would go on to serve as Darwin's editor and proofreader on later projects. The two-volume *The Descent of Man, and Selection in Relation to Sex* appeared in 1871.

With *Descent of Man* Darwin finally dealt with human origins directly, as well as with human relationships to other animals, and expanded his concept of sexual selection, which he had introduced but not detailed in *On the Origin of Species*. Although Darwin supported the Victorian view that differences existed between so-called savages and civilized humans, he argued that human races graduated one into another. At the time there were considerable disagreements between those who argued that there were multiple human species or at least races that arose from separate ancestors.

This was the concept of polygenesis as opposed to monogenesis, which argued that all humans share a common ancestor. The debate included a tangle of religious and scientific arguments. The biblical account of Adam and Eve argued for monogenesis – that the races arose from the sons of Noah following the biblical Flood – whereas others argued that most races other than the ones leading to Europeans were pre-Adamite. Some naturalists such as the American geologist Louis Agassiz, an avowed anti-evolutionist, argued for the presence of at least three supposed major races, indicating at least three different origins of humans. Others, such as the German evolutionary naturalist Ernst Haeckel, argued for many more origins. Although a diehard Darwin acolyte, Haeckel parted company with Darwin on the question of human origins. Darwin was firmly in the monogenic camp, as were many of his other supporters and even detractors such as Richard Owen. The fact that fertile offspring occurred between members of different races was proof that humans form a single species descended from a common ancestor. The increased antiquity of the human fossils being discovered added strength to the monogenic argument.

Darwin never pointedly wrote that humans were descended from monkeys or apes but rather placed humans among the primates, further stressing humans as of and not above nature and correctly presuming that Africa was the place of origin of humankind. He even made sketches of his ideas on human evolution gleaned from the work of others, but he never published any of them. One from 1868 in particular is probably the last kind of tree sketch we know he drew. This was an elaborate evolutionary tree of primates, not just of human origins. At first glance, the figure appears very messy and even haphazardly drawn. Examining it more closely, it becomes clear that Darwin changed his mind several times and scratched out portions, overwriting names of various primate groups. In what can be discerned as the final version, he shows a cluster of three branches, one labelled 'gorilla and chimp', the second labelled 'orangutan', and the third *Hylobates* (gibbon). The next closest branch is labelled 'Man'. He was clearly indicating that other apes are the nearest relatives of humans, not human ancestors.[10]

Darwin did not only take a keen interest in human origins. He also pondered and wrote about the origins of other domestic animals, notably pigeons, chickens and, especially, dogs, starting in *On the Origin of Species*. In the case of pigeons, Darwin's own breeding experiments at Down House had convinced him along with most other naturalists that all the fancy breeds of domestic pigeons had descended through selective breeding from the wild rock pigeon. Darwin argued that all the breeds of domestic chicken likewise had a single source, arguing for the red jungle fowl on the Indian subcontinent. He was right about the red jungle fowl, although there may have been interbreeding along the way with wild species and the place of origin may be in the northern parts of Southeast Asia or southern China.[11]

Dogs held a special place in Darwin's heart, so it is no wonder that he became interested in the origin of the many, varied breeds. Unlike for the case of humans, pigeons and chickens for which he argued a single origin, Darwin argued that different breeds of dogs arose from several species of the canid or dog family. Thomas Bell, the man who had described Darwin's reptiles and amphibians in *The Zoology of the Voyage of HMS Beagle* in the early 1840s, had taken a different view in an 1837 book in which he noted that the grey wolf and the domestic dog can interbreed with fertile offspring and that the two have a similar length of gestation of 63 days. Thus, the likely single origin for dogs was the grey wolf. Even the geologist Charles Lyell tried to convince Darwin on the basis of Bell's work of the single origin of dogs, but Darwin would not be moved, arguing more strongly over the years that the great diversity of dog breeds called for multiple origins. We know today that Bell and Lyell were correct and Darwin wrong.

Darwin had taken a special interest in dogs and their ancestry because he had owned many over the years. His probable favourite was a terrier named Polly, originally owned by his daughter Henrietta. Polly was acquired in summer 1871, around the time *Descent of Man* came out. Polly became Darwin's dog when Henrietta married and moved to London with her new husband Richard Buckley Litchfield. In this newly published volume, Darwin discussed what he regarded as the moral sense and loyalty that dogs can show their masters, to the point of arguing that dogs could recall times that they had misbehaved. He noted that the various breeds had been selected by humans over time to perform specific tasks – the greyhound for speed and the pointer for finding and indicating prey.

It was not until *The Descent of Man* that Darwin fully developed his theory of sexual selection. He wrote in this work how natural selection and sexual selection would reinforce one another. He recognized two kinds of sexual selection, which are not mutually exclusive and which we today call male-male competition and mate choice. Although not exclusively restricted to males, it is most commonly males who develop secondary sexual characteristics that either can be used in male-male competition or to win a mate. The Victorian readers of Darwin could more easily accept male-male competition, since they witnessed how the larger size of males or the presence of horns, antlers or canine teeth could be used for intimidation or actual battles. The victor successfully mates, while the vanquished is forced to retreat. How and why mate choice – in which the male must woo the female to successfully mate – would work was less understood. For Darwin, physical displays, songs and elaborate ornamentation could be explained only by the fact of the male evolving over time more and more ornate means to attract a female. He was especially perplexed by the extravagant tail of the male peacock, remarking in a letter to Asa Gray that 'the sight of a feather in a peacock's tail, whenever I gaze at it, makes me sick.'[12]

With further study he showed that although such a tail could be a potential advertisement for a predator, this was outweighed by its need to successfully attract a mate. The females would select the males with the more sumptuous features or elaborate displays, thus reinforcing these traits over continued generations. In addition to the possibility of the female selecting a male simply because of his appeal to her, that same appeal might also indicate the superior health of that individual, a fact of which the female was probably oblivious. Mate choice did not find a ready audience in patriarchal Victorian England.

Regarding the importance and meaning of sexual selection, the co-discoverer of natural selection Alfred Russel Wallace begged to differ with Darwin. Wallace argued that natural selection was much more important in the development of secondary sexual characteristics than sexual selection. He thought that this was especially true for colours in birds and insects. Wallace argued that the extravagant plumage colours developing in male birds did not arise through female mate choice, but rather that females had evolved their dull colours via natural selection as a form of protection while nesting. The two never fully agreed, but they compromised: Darwin accepted that Wallace was right about natural selection leading to protective coloration, but still argued of the importance of sexual selection in animals, including humans.

Because Darwin delayed in publishing about human ancestry, he was beaten to the punch by Huxley's *Man's Place in Nature* and Lyell's *Geological Evidences of the Antiquity of Man*, both appearing in 1863. One positive aspect of this delay was that these earlier works softened the blow when Darwin's book finally appeared. People were already primed to hear about how humans had descended from lower species. A negative for Darwin regarding Lyell's book on human antiquity was that Lyell still remained only lukewarm to Darwin's evolutionary theory, notably when it came to natural selection. The closest Lyell ever came to supporting Darwin's descent with modification by means of natural selection, at least in print, would be in later editions of his *Principles of Geology*.

In 1867 Darwin circulated to colleagues and friends a printed leaflet titled 'Queries about Expression', which included sixteen questions about facial expressions and related emotions in the human face in reaction to various stimuli. He would use results from this questionnaire as part of his final work, which arose from writings in his 'big book' manuscript. This book, published in 1872, was *The Expression of the Emotions in Man and Animals*, in which he related how both humans and animals shared similarly evolved reactions to stimuli. As she had done the year earlier with *The Descent of Man*, Darwin's daughter Henrietta was of considerable help in checking, along with her brother Leonard, the book's proofs. The book sold almost 7,000 copies and received good reviews.

This was the only one of his books to include photographs. These images, documenting human facial expressions, were produced using the new heliotype method, which employed a photomechanical process to produce a plate by exposing a gelatine film under a negative, hardening it with chrome alum, and printing directly from it. His publisher John Murray noted that the extra cost would adversely affect profits, but Darwin insisted on including the images as he thought the heliotypes were better at showing what he wished to demonstrate about human facial expressions. Darwin had actors imitate various emotions, while babies and children were also depicted expressing emotions, and he borrowed work from the French physician and neurology pioneer Duchenne de Boulogne, who employed the method of electrical stimuli to elicit facial expressions in volunteers. Important to Darwin was the refutation of the then-popular belief that the expressive facial muscles in humans were specially endowed by God. Darwin used illustrations of various animals to make the genetic and thus evolutionary link with human expressions

A man expressing terror, based on a photograph in *The Expression of the Emotions*.

of emotion, showing that those found in humans first arose in animals. The universality of expression in humans, whether 'primitive' or 'civilized' people, supported his argument for a common ancestry of all humans.

Darwin had now mostly accomplished the goal he had set himself in the 1850s of bringing his 'big book' to fruition, but he was not yet ready to rest on his laurels. Instead he now turned his scientific attentions more fully to botany, still with the idea that these studies would bring support of his theories on evolution.

10

Teasing Plants and Tending Worms

The considerable success of the orchid book in 1862 anticipated what would be the remainder of Darwin's new scientific endeavours and his life. He was of course busy rewriting and producing new editions of his seminal works on evolution, but with his 'big book' published in four different works by 1872, Darwin turned to more botanically centred research. Even with the critical success of his orchid book we seldom consider Darwin to be a botanist, yet during his life he published no fewer than six books on botanical topics (including his already published book on orchids and his monograph on climbing plants). Certainly a major influence in his decision to delve more deeply into botany came from two of his closest botanical friends, Hooker in England and Gray in America. Plants now became the centrepiece of his research, and although not specifically used as proof of his evolutionary theorizing the study of them was nonetheless supportive of this end.

Darwin conducted much of his botanical experimentation and observation in the greenhouse he had built at Down House between 1855 and 1856. It started out as a lean-to structure next to the boundary wall bordering the kitchen garden but became more sophisticated over the years, notably with a hothouse added in 1863 which sported the newest technology of a coke-fired stove for heating water that circulated in pipes around the small structure. Thus his area to grow plants was no longer limited by the changeable and often inclement weather of Great Britain. At the

The greenhouse at Down House.

time of Darwin's death in 1882 there were reportedly three or four sections to the greenhouse complex. These facilities had become important for his experiments on his beloved orchids, studying various aspects of plant growth as well as variations in the forms of flowers, fertilization patterns and the carnivory of plants, which he termed insectivory. On the opposite side of the wall from the greenhouse complex a brick structure was erected in 1881, not long before Darwin's death. There is little evidence that he ever utilized this structure, which was variously known as the shed or laboratory.

One of his first botanical tasks was to retool his rather dry monograph on climbing plants published in the *Journal of the Linnean Society* in 1865 into a book to be published by John Murray. The inspiration for the original monograph had come about after reading a paper by Gray on how plant tendrils would coil upwardly in their quest to find purchase on a supporting structure. Gray spurred Darwin's interest even more when he sent over seeds of the wild cucumber native to northeastern North America. Darwin was mesmerized by how the tendrils reacted to touch in their search for a holdfast. His publisher John Murray realized that the reading public would not be enthralled with the topic of climbing plants, so at only 1,500 first-run copies this was probably the smallest of any press run for a Darwin book.

In 1875, the year that *Climbing Plants* came out, Darwin's quite delightful book *Insectivorous Plants* also appeared, but this time Murray had planned a larger print run as the topic of how plants could consume insects held a more fascinating, somewhat morbid curiosity for the public. Darwin had been experimenting with these plants for at least fifteen years by this point. The several sorts of plants he studied included those, like the common sundew and the pitcher plant, that more passively ensnare their victims in a sticky substance or possess a slippery edge that causes prey to fall into a liquid-filled vessel in which it is then dissolved. More active prey capture occurs in the Venus flytrap, which has two halves that snap shut, entrapping its victim. Darwin theorized that these plants could survive in nitrogen-poor environments such as peat bogs because they had evolved mechanisms to extract nutrients they required from prey. He tried all manner of perturbations of poking, prodding, teasing and blowing on the plants as well as feeding them everything from meat to glass. He enlisted physiologist colleagues who could help him understand the chemical processes involved. He even had his sons Francis and George, now young men, prepare some of the illustrations for the book. While not a major evolutionary work, it nonetheless provided yet more evidence for Darwin's growing body of proof that showed how species evolved by adapting to their environmental conditions under the forces of natural selection.

Francis Darwin, Darwin and Emma's seventh child, began his studies at the University of Cambridge in the physical sciences but changed to the natural sciences. He then earned a degree in medicine from St George's Medical School in 1875, but during this time his passion for botany flourished, leading him to help his father at Down House. Francis also visited and learned at more recently established laboratories, especially in Germany, where he became familiar with the most current techniques in plant physiology. Here the latest equipment and techniques, which were lacking at Down House, were being used in experimental botany. He tried to bring his father around to the newer approaches, but only with a modicum of success. Darwin's background as a gentleman-scientist made him stubbornly resistant to the advances occurring in botany. This resulted in the view that he was a natural historian mired in the old ways rather than accepting of the newer, more rigorous experimental approaches. This meant that even when he provided intriguing and often correct results in plant reproduction and physiology, his lack of more modern approaches hindered the acceptance of his work. Francis supported his father's work, but probably felt frustrated.

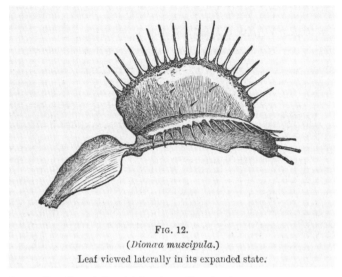

An open Venus flytrap in Darwin's *Insectivorous Plants* (1875).

During this time Darwin reluctantly found himself immersed in the public controversy then raging over vivisection – the operating on live animals for scientific purposes. Opinions ran the gamut from the strident belief that no experimentation should be conducted on live animals to the view that experimentation was allowable only if no pain was inflicted, and finally to the idea that the animal could be experimented on irrespective of the pain inflicted. Although a hunter and collector of animal specimens, Darwin regarded himself as an animal-lover. He found himself conflicted. He responded in a letter to a colleague that 'I quite agree that it is justifiable for real investigations on physiology; but not for mere damnable and detestable curiosity. It is a subject which makes me sick with horror, so I will not say another word about it, else I shall not sleep to-night.'[1] He had also related in *The Descent of Man* that such experimentation must have justification and that the experimenter may experience remorse for his actions until his last days.

The controversy came to a head in England in August 1874. At a medical meeting in Norwich, the invited French physiologist Eugene Magnan intravenously injected alcohol and absinthe into dogs to induce epilepsy. The audience was outraged, with the president of the Royal College of Surgeons even freeing one of the dogs. The county magistrates were called and charges brought against those involved in the exhibition, but at the trial in December 1874 the English organizers were found not guilty of taking part in the experiment. A month following the trial Darwin was asked to sign a petition circulated by Frances Power Cobbe that garnered over six hundred signatures calling on the Royal Society for the Prevention of Cruelty to Animals to investigate all animal experimentation and to draft legislation to stop it. Darwin declined to sign, finding the language of the proposed measure inflammatory. Under the counsel of his son-in-law Richard Buckley Litchfield, he helped to draft a proposal that set forth why vivisection was important to physiological and medical research – but he still rejected work that needlessly inflicted pain on animals. None of these competing bills, including the version Darwin helped draft, passed Parliament in 1875, but the next year a Royal Commission was established to investigate vivisection. Darwin was one of 53 witnesses called by the commission to testify. In his statement he emphasized that progress in physiology was possible only with the aid of experiments on living animals, but that the animals must be rendered insensible to pain. When asked what his view was on 'trying a painful experiment without anaesthetics, when the same experiment could be made with anaesthetics . . . what would be your view on that subject?' Darwin responded: 'It deserves detestation and abhorrence.'[2]

Personal involvement in public matters always vexed Darwin, especially when it involved his own work. As he grew older, such endeavours exacerbated his various illnesses. He found solace in his plants and was soon back among them, this time preparing his next book, published in late 1876, dealing with, as the title explains, *The Effects of Cross and Self Fertilisation in the Vegetable Kingdom*. In more than sixty plant species Francis provided microscope work that helped his father show differences in survival between plants that cross-pollinated between different individuals versus those that pollinated within the same individual. Darwin discovered that the self-fertilizing plants did more poorly. Today we refer to the results that Darwin found as 'inbreeding depression'. Although this was suspected, Darwin could not demonstrate why this was the case. As with many of his findings, years passed before an adequate explanation emerged. He intended these results to be complementary to his work on orchids and certainly they enforced the same views he espoused in *On the Origin of Species* on the importance of cross-breeding versus inbreeding for the survival of a species.

The year 1876 proved both momentous and tragic for the Darwin family. Amy Ruck Darwin, wife of Francis, gave birth to Bernard, Charles and Emma's first grandchild. Within four days Amy died of a fever, possibly related to the birth. The devastated Francis moved into Down House with his infant son. Amy had been a particular friend and confidante of the Darwins' youngest daughter and sixth child Elizabeth 'Bessy', who was only three years Amy's senior. Unlike her sister Henrietta but more similar to Amy, Elizabeth was quiet and reserved, in part as a result of some developmental problems, at least while a child. As an adult, she was interested in education and women's issues, notably suffrage, activities she shared with her sister Henrietta. We know little of her other than she never married and always lived in the family home at Downe and then with her mother Emma in Cambridge until Emma's death in 1896. Her nephew Bernard wrote fondly of his Aunt Bessy in his autobiography. Bernard would go on to make a name for himself as a golf writer. His father would marry two more times: first in 1883 to Ellen Wordsworth Crofts, with whom he had a daughter, Frances Crofts Darwin, who became a poet known under her married name, Frances Cornford; when Ellen died, he married his third wife Florence Henrietta Fisher.

Perhaps sensing his own mortality, Darwin wrote a short *Autobiography* intended only for his children and grandchildren. Although not written for public consumption, Francis published it in 1887 with the help of his sister Henrietta, five years after their father's death, as part of a volume titled *The Life and Letters of Charles Darwin, including an Autobiographical Chapter*. Unfortunately, they took it upon themselves to expunge any passages deemed critical of God and Christianity. Only in 1958 did Darwin's granddaughter Nora Barlow, daughter of Horace Darwin, replace the missing passages in an anniversary version celebrating the one-hundredth anniversary of the publication of *On the Origin of Species*. Henrietta also edited and published letters of her mother Emma, first privately in 1904 as *Emma Darwin, Wife of Charles Darwin: A Century of Family* and then more widely in 1915.

Darwin's next botanical book (and fifth of six he would publish), released in 1877, was *The Different Forms of Flowers on Plants of the Same Species*. As with his other botanical books this work comprised a compilation of papers that he had written for the Linnean Society. He dedicated the work to Asa Gray, 'as a small tribute of respect and affection'. This was the second and final time he included a book dedication, the first to Charles Lyell more than thirty years prior in the second edition of *Journal of Researches*. This rarity argues for just how high in his esteem he held these two men. Francis once again helped his father with the experiments and wrote the preface for the second edition published two years after his father's death. Darwin realized while writing it that this book was too technical and dry for the general public. In his *Autobiography* Darwin commented that although very few people appreciated this work, he was nevertheless very pleased with his discoveries relating to heterostylous plants, those plants in which the female reproductive parts in the flower, the style, may vary in size and form in different individuals of the same species. Darwin wanted to determine if there were differences in reproductive success between crossings of individuals with different flower morphology. His experiments found that indeed there are differences in reproductive success even to the point of some crosses resulting in sterility. This probably sparked his thinking on how existing species might split to form new ones, as sterility would help to divert populations into two distinct breeding groups.

Later in the same year of 1877 Darwin received an accolade that pleased him greatly. In November his alma mater, the University of Cambridge, conferred upon him an honorary LL.D. or Doctor of Laws. The University of Oxford had almost beaten Cambridge at the post, in 1870 offering to confer upon Darwin a DCL or Doctor of Civil Law. Darwin had to decline then because of ill health and was afraid that he might also need to decline this time as well. He made it to Cambridge accompanied by wife Emma, sons Leonard and Horace, daughter Henrietta, and perhaps George and Francis. It was an elaborate ceremony with all principals bedecked in scarlet robes and what seemed like interminable speeches. Levity came in the form of a stuffed monkey in academic robes suspended from the rafters, which was deliberately intended to evoke Darwin's work on human origins. Irreverence was provided by outbursts among unruly undergraduates.

In 1879, to commemorate Darwin's honorary degree, the Cambridge Philosophical Society solicited £400 from Cambridge graduates to have William Blake Richmond paint a portrait of Darwin seated in the scarlet academic robes of the investiture. On a visit to Cambridge in October 1881, upon seeing the portrait, Emma wrote, 'We went to see the picture, and I thought it quite horrid, so fierce and so dirty.'[3] Perhaps Emma's criticism is too harsh, because this is only one of very few images of Darwin in which he bears just a hint of a bemused cat-eating-the-canary smile. He deserved some modicum of self-satisfaction.

Darwin's final plant book, *The Power of Movement in Plants*, appeared in 1880, two years before his death. This time he more directly acknowledged the experimental contributions of Francis by placing his name below his own on the title page as an assistant. One could say Francis was co-author in all but name. As with his other specialist books, it did not sell well; in fact this was the least successful of any of his books and it did not appear in revised editions. The book continued his work on plant movement that had been initiated in *Climbing Plants*. It showed how plants respond to various external stimuli, extending Darwin's ideas of how natural selection helps govern growth and survival. By the end of the nineteenth century the phenomena Darwin observed came to be known as tropisms, which are defined as involuntary positive or negative responses of an organism or its parts to external stimuli. It can occur in sedentary animals or plants, but Darwin was only studying responses in plants. There are any number of tropisms, but two that Darwin were especially interested in examining were heliotropism and phototropism, reactions to sunshine and to light, respectively. A specific example was Darwin's interest in the response of grass seedlings as they bend and grow towards the light.

In the midst of finishing these last two books on plants, Darwin turned his hand to biography, or more accurately writing the preface to a biography of his grandfather Erasmus Darwin. In the end he found himself embroiled in a quite senseless controversy. It began innocently enough with an issue of the German journal *Kosmos* honouring Darwin's seventieth birthday. The issue included an article by Ernst Krause on the history of evolutionary theory and the influence of Darwin's grandfather Erasmus. Krause expanded the article into a book that Darwin had translated into English to which Darwin contributed what he called a 'Preliminary Notice'. It certainly was not preliminary in most senses of the word because, of the 217 pages that composed Krause's *Life of Erasmus Darwin*, Darwin contributed 127, which his daughter Henrietta helped edit.

The controversy began when the – at first cordial – correspondence between Samuel Butler, the author of *Erewhon*, and Darwin soured over Butler's claim that Darwin had not given due credit to his grandfather Erasmus and Lamarck for their evolutionary ideas. In that same year, 1879, Butler published his book on this topic titled *Evolution, Old and New; or, The Theories of Buffon, Dr Erasmus Darwin, and Lamarck, as Compared with that of Mr Charles Darwin*. Butler accused Darwin and Krause of disparaging and purloining his work. The whole kerfuffle came to naught, but predictably took its toll on Darwin. The irony was that this Samuel Butler was the grandson of the Samuel Butler who headed the Shrewsbury School that Darwin had attended as a boy and which he held in very low regard.

For what would prove to be his last book, Darwin now turned to a subject that he had first investigated and written about some forty years earlier – the actions of earthworms that produce much of the humus we find in soils in many parts of the world. In 1837, not long after returning from his voyage on the *Beagle*, Darwin presented a paper at the Geological Society of London titled 'On the Formation of Mould' which discussed how earthworms process earth. The *Transactions of the Geological Society* published this paper the next year based on this talk.[4] Darwin's interest in the subject never went away. This topic bridged biology and geology in what today we would call the science of ecology. This science examines the relationships of organisms to each other and to their environment. The word derives from the Greek words for 'house' (*oikos*) and 'study of' (*logos*) and was coined in 1866 by the German biologist Ernst Haeckel, an acolyte of Darwin.

Darwin is not thought of as an ecologist but much of his work drew from the field, especially as it impacts his evolutionary work. In *On the Origin of Species* in 1859 he referred to the economy or polity of nature, essentially in the same sense as ecology. Darwin explained the interrelationships in nature as told by a story 'showing how plants and animals, most remote in the scale of nature, are bound together by a web of complex relations'. One of his most poetic and insightful cases dealt with cats, field mice, humblebees and red clover to show how nature forms a complex web of relations. We now know humblebees as bumblebees, a gradual twentieth-century shift, but they earned their original name from the humming they create as they fly. Darwin experimented and found that the humblebees were important if not vital to the fertilization of red clover, an important forage plant for grazers. Other sorts of bees and insects simply lacked the appropriate mouth parts needed to reach the nectar. He found that the number of humblebees in any district depended on the numbers of field mice because the latter destroy the combs and nests of the humblebees. The number of field mice depends upon the resident cat population. Thus, when more cats are present there are fewer field mice and more humblebees and hence more red clover. In the next paragraph he made the more general observation that the distributions of plants in what he liked to refer to as the 'entangled bank' may look random but is anything but, as there are clear checks and balances at play creating what we see.[5] Darwin can rightfully be called one of the founders of ecology.

Darwin's lifelong interest in the action of earthworms led him to all manner of experiments. He had pots scattered about the house containing worms upon which he performed various experiments. Among their food preferences, raw carrots proved a favourite. At night he subjected them to strong light, which made them head for their burrows. He played various sounds to little effect: he shouted at them, played a whistle, had his son Francis's bassoon played loudly and set them close to a piano, though upon striking keys there was no effect. However, when they were placed upon the piano and keys were struck the worms did react to the vibrations.

Caricature of Darwin in *Punch* titled 'Politic Worm',
22 October 1881.

Darwin placed a heavy, flat stone on the lawn at Down House to
note the actions of the worms as they began to bury the edges of the
stone. Based upon such experiments as the worm stone, Darwin
calculated that more than 50,000 worms per acre recycle the soil.
As noted previously, the original worm stone disappeared, but
Horace, the ninth child of Emma and Charles, had his company
reconstruct a replica, which was placed at Down House in 1929
and still survives today. In 1881 Horace, who had earned his degree
in civil engineering at the University of Cambridge, co-founded a
firm, the Cambridge Scientific Instrument Company. In addition
to his reputation as a well-respected businessman, Horace served

as mayor of Cambridge between 1896 and 1897. He married Emma Cecilia Farrer in 1880, with whom he had a son and two daughters.

This worm work resulted in Darwin's last book, published six months before his death. *The Formation of Vegetable Mould Through the Action of Worms, with Observations on Their Habits* (1881) proved a captivating and non-controversial topic for the agriculturally inclined British and thus the book sold well, faster in fact than the original publication of *On the Origin of Species*. It sold 6,000 copies within the first year, and as many as 13,000 by the end of the nineteenth century. It was written in a manner easily accessible to many readers and a style that highlighted Darwin's love of nature. Because of his fame and the popularity of the book the satirical journal *Punch* published an illustration of an old, contemplative Darwin sitting in a garden musing upon a giant worm arched above his head in the shape of a question mark. The caption reads that Darwin 'has lately been turning his attention to the "Politic Worm"'.

11

Not the Least Afraid of Death

Charles Robert Darwin's health was in decline for almost three months in early 1882 as he suffered from complications of heart disease. He succumbed at Down House on 19 April, aged 73 and surrounded by family. It is reported that his last words to Emma were 'I am not the least afraid of death. Remember what a good wife you have been to me. Tell all my children to remember how good they have been to me.'[1]

The Australian-born British Christian evangelist Elizabeth Cotton, Lady Hope, promulgated a grotesque urban legend in the early twentieth century concerning a deathbed recantation by Darwin. When she first told her story in 1915, she had been living in the United States for several years. She claimed to have visited Darwin shortly before his death and that he had expressed doubts about his theory of evolution by means of natural selection, and further that he wished to express to a gathering that Jesus Christ was his salvation. This was first published in the *Watchman-Examiner* in Boston.[2] Although this weekly published some secular news, its primary purpose was to provide religious reports, and Darwin's comments were a sensation. Darwin's children debunked the account. Francis Darwin wrote that 'Lady Hope's account of my father's views on religion is quite untrue. I have publicly accused her of falsehood.' Henrietta, who was with her father at his death, stated that Lady Hope had not visited, at least at that time, declaring Hope's story a complete fabrication. She stated that

Charles and Emma in old age, 1881.

her father 'never recanted any of his scientific views, either then or earlier. We think the story of his conversion was fabricated in the USA.' Leonard Darwin called Hope's account 'purely fictitious' and a 'hallucination'. [3] Fake news may make the rounds much more rapidly today because of the Internet but such tropes have an ancient pedigree.

Darwin's religious beliefs changed dramatically throughout his life. As he wrote in his *Autobiography*, as a young man he did not have the least doubt of the 'strict and literal truth of every word in the Bible'. [4] He even contemplated continuing his Cambridge education after earning his undergraduate degree in order to obtain a theological degree that would allow him to become a parson in a quiet country parish. There he could follow his natural history pursuits as time permitted. When Darwin truly began to study nature and not simply dabble in it, the human perception of savagery in nature – Alfred, Lord Tennyson's 'Nature, red in tooth and claw'[5] – began to seriously make him doubt the benevolence of a deity. In a letter to Asa Gray he wrote that he could not persuade himself that a 'beneficent and omnipotent God' existed if He had created the parasitic ichneumonid wasp, which lays its eggs in living caterpillars only to have the larvae eat the living caterpillar from the inside out.[6] The death of his much beloved ten-year-old daughter Annie in 1851 was the final straw for his religious beliefs.

The truth of Darwin's religious beliefs near the end of his life come to us from a letter he wrote in 1880. On 23 November 1880 Francis McDermott, a young barrister at the time, wrote that he took great pleasure from Darwin's books but by doing so he did not wish to lose his faith in the New Testament. He asked Darwin to give him a yes or no answer as to whether the famous naturalist believed in the New Testament. Darwin responded succinctly that he was 'sorry to have to inform' McDermott that he 'did not believe in the Bible as a divine revelation and therefore not in Jesus Christ as the son of God'. Darwin jotted at the top of the letter the underlined word 'Private'.[7] McDermott honoured the request; his letter only becoming widely known at an auction in New York City in September 2015 when it sold for almost $200,000.

There is little doubt that because of his work on the origin of species by means of natural selection, which Darwin espoused in his 1859 seminal book, he was denied a knighthood or any other state recognition, mostly through the efforts of ecclesiastical officials such as Bishop Wilberforce. Knighthoods or other state honours were bestowed on many of his contemporaries, friends and adversaries alike, such as J. D. Hooker, Richard Owen, Charles Lyell, Alfred Wallace, T. H. Huxley and three of his five sons: Francis, George and Horace. This list makes it very clear that he was intentionally denied such honours. His seminal work made him far too controversial at the time for the Church of England, headed by Queen Victoria, to recognize him in such a public fashion. In the ensuing years after *On the Origin of Species* appeared, views had softened towards his theory and there was even a measured degree of acceptance beyond the scientific community. It only took the Church of England 150 years to offer a direct if rather pointless apology to the long-dead Darwin in 2008 for the sesquicentennial of the publication of the work. An article written by a Church official, Malcolm Brown, in part reads that the 'Church of England owes you an apology for misunderstanding you and, by getting our first reaction wrong, encouraging others to misunderstand you still.' This was to their shame but was rectified to some extent upon Darwin's death.[8]

Darwin wished to be buried in the churchyard of St Mary's, the Church of England Parish in the village of Downe where other Darwins preceded him in death – his children Mary Eleanor and Charles Waring, and brother Ras. Emma would follow them in 1896, as would several other children, spouses and grandchildren each in their time. A groundswell of support led by Darwin's colleagues began very soon after his death to have him buried in Westminster Abbey, arguably the most honoured place of burial in Great Britain. Bishop Wilberforce had been dead almost ten years and could not demur about Darwin's burial at Westminster. Since the Middle Ages British monarchs, such as Henry v and all the Tudors except Henry viii, had been interred there. Also buried or memorialized in the abbey are clergy, authors, artists, statesmen, musicians, actors and scientists, Stephen Hawking most recently in 2018, whose ashes were interred between the graves of Isaac Newton and Charles Darwin.

Parliament had to be petitioned to allow a burial at Westminster Abbey, but there was such broad public support that a second snub of the great man by the Church and government was easily thwarted. George Granville Bradley, Dean of Westminster Abbey, was away in France at the time. There he received a forwarded telegram from the president of the Royal Society, William Spottiswoode, reading in part that 'it would be acceptable to a very large number of our fellow-countrymen of all classes and opinions

Funeral of Darwin in Westminster Abbey, 1882.

that our illustrious countryman, Mr Darwin, should be buried in
Westminster Abbey.' Bradley recalled that he did not have the least
hesitation in granting the request and offered his cheerful assent.[9]

Because of the anticipated thousands who might attend the
funeral, various sorts of tickets were issued to permit admittance
to different parts of the abbey. *The Times* noted that a large number
of people without tickets were allowed into the north-side nave.
Dignitaries from the embassies of Italy, Spain, Germany and
France attended as did many academics from around Great Britain.
Ironically, unlike foreign countries that had bestowed various
honours on Darwin while he was alive, his own government had
not done so, but it could now make belated amends.

The funeral and interment were arranged for 26 April, a week
after Darwin died. Darwin's body lay overnight in the small
chapel of St Faith, and on the morning of 26 April the coffin was
escorted by the family and eminent mourners into the abbey. The
service was held in the lantern with the choir singing chorales
composed especially for the funeral. *The Times* reported that at
11.40 a.m. Darwin's body was brought from the chapel into the west
cloister, where the procession was formed. The coffin was draped

in black velvet upon which were laid many wreaths of beautiful white flowers. The eldest Darwin son, William, served as chief mourner attended by other members of the family. Pallbearers included the close scientific friends Hooker, Huxley, Wallace, friends and neighbours William Spottiswoode and John Lubbock, the American ambassador to the United Kingdom James Russell Lowell, and members of the peerage: George Campbell (9th Duke of Argyll), William Cavendish (7th Duke of Devonshire) and Edward Henry Stanley (15th Earl of Derby).

A Carrara marble slab covers Darwin's grave in the floor in the north aisle of the nave of the abbey. Friend and mentor Charles Lyell had been buried there in 1875. Darwin's grave is quite close to the elaborate tomb of Isaac Newton and immediately adjacent to that of the astronomer John Herschel, the same man who had written about changes in species being 'that mystery of mysteries' which Darwin had later quoted at the beginning of his magnum opus. Herschel's inscription is quite elaborate; Darwin's simply reads, 'Charles Robert Darwin Born 12 February 1809 Died 19 April 1882.' Darwin's family had a life-sized relief bust set within a circular medallion installed near the grave in 1888, reading simply DARWIN.

Unique busts, medallions and statues of Darwin number in the hundreds, with perhaps thousands of copies scattered around the world. Arguably the most famous and storied is by Joseph Edgar Boehm, of a seated, bearded, older Darwin positioned on the landing of the main hall stairwell at the Natural History Museum, London. Its planning began shortly after Darwin's death. In 1885 Huxley unveiled the statue to considerable fanfare – the Prince of Wales was even in attendance. The scene was captured by *The Graphic*, a British weekly illustrated newspaper. Even the founder and first director of the museum, and now Darwin's adversary, Richard Owen, begrudgingly admitted to the powerful museum trustee Spencer Walpole that Darwin merited a statute in the Natural History Museum. In 1897, a year after Owen's death, a

Statue of Darwin in the Natural History Museum, London, and its unveiling, 1885.

bronze statue of a standing Owen clutching the femur of the large extinct New Zealand bird *Dinornis* was erected in the main hall opposite Darwin. Accounts vary but supposedly in 1927 Darwin was first replaced by an elephant and then by the statue of Owen. Darwin's statue had been moved out of the main hall from its original position. In anticipation of the 200th anniversary of Darwin's birth and the 150th anniversary of the publication of *On the Origin of Species* in 2009 his statue was moved back to its original position, while that of Owen is now on the landing upstairs from Darwin.

The awards and honours Darwin received during his life were numerous and varied. Beginning in 1826 the Royal Society awarded two Royal Medals each year for 'distinguished contributions in the applied sciences' and to 'the most important contributions to the advancement of natural knowledge'. In 1853 John Tyndall won it for physics and as noted earlier, Charles Darwin won it in natural history for his books on coral reefs, volcanic islands, the geology of South America, and his works on living and fossil barnacles. This recognition meant a great deal to Darwin. In 1859 he was awarded the Wollaston Medal, the highest award of the Geological Society of London.

In 1864 George Busk accepted the Copley Medal on behalf of Darwin, which Darwin received 'for his important researches in geology, zoology, and botanical physiology', but nothing on the citation noted his world-shaking *On the Origin of Species*, published only five years earlier. In fact, because of considerable objection to his evolution work, Darwin's award of the Copley Medal required strong advocacy by the X Club. This group had been started as a dining club in 1864 by Thomas Henry Huxley with the purpose of supporting academic liberalism generally and Charles Darwin's theory of natural selection specifically. The nine-member group, in addition to Huxley, included George Busk, Edward Frankland, Thomas Archer Hirst, Joseph Dalton Hooker, John Lubbock,

Herbert Spencer, William Spottiswoode and John Tyndall. After several attempts at naming the group, 'X Club' was chosen in 1865, according to Herbert Spencer because it committed the group to nothing; the only rule was that the group was to have no rules. Individually and as a group these men were influential, hoping to reform the Royal Society so as to add greater emphasis to the profession of science.

In 1870 the University of Oxford wished to award Darwin an honorary DCL, or Doctor of Civil Law, but it was never conferred because ill health prevented him from attending the ceremony, and thus the degree was never bestowed. As described earlier, the University of Cambridge had conferred upon Darwin an honorary LL.D., or Doctor of Laws, in 1877, which he greatly relished and included after his name in all future publications. In 1879 the Royal College of Physicians presented Darwin with the biennially awarded Baly Medal for work in physiology.

In addition to honours within the United Kingdom and its colonies of Australia, India and New Zealand, Darwin also received various accolades from around the world. In 1868 he was made a knight of the Prussian order Pour le Mérite. In 1879 he received the Bressa Prize of the Royal Academy of Turin. Additionally, he received honorary degrees from Breslau, Bonn and Leiden, as well as being elected to many other foreign scientific societies in Argentina, Austria-Hungary, Belgium, Denmark, France, Germany, the Netherlands, Italy, Portugal, Russia, Spain, Sweden, Switzerland and the United States.[10]

The greatest legacy of Darwin rests not with the honours he received but rather with his status as the pre-eminent scientist who proved evolution and provided its primary mechanism. This eminent position was not always the case. When Darwin died in 1882 his theory of evolution by means of natural selection suffered a decline in acceptance among scientists for two primary reasons. First, there was still no way to demonstrate that Earth was extremely ancient, and, according to Darwin's theory, evolution required expansive amounts of time over which to occur. This would be solved near the beginning of the twentieth century. In 1898 two-time Nobel Prize-winning scientist Marie Curie discovered radioactivity, the process by which atoms decay and emit a form of energy called radiation. By 1904 the New Zealand-born British physicist Ernest Rutherford showed that radioactive decay occurs in rocks that had once been molten, thus allowing the geological age at which the rock cooled to be determined. This then might provide various ages for events in Earth's history, which the then young British geologist Arthur Holmes explained in the journal *Nature* in 1913 using the process of decay from uranium to lead. He estimated Earth to be 1.6 billion years old. He commented in the *Nature* article, 'The geologist who ten years ago was embarrassed by the shortness of time allowed to him for the evolution of the Earth's crust, is still more embarrassed with the superabundance with which he is now confronted.'[11] Physicist William Thomson was wrong, and Darwin was correct. Earth is very old, and in its history there has been ample time for evolution. Although debate among geologists continued for some time, today there is no debate – Earth has existed for about 4.56 billion years.

The second and even greater problem with Darwin's theory pervaded the large University of Cambridge centenary celebration of Darwin's birth and fiftieth anniversary of the publication of *On the Origin of Species* in 1909. Darwin's great masterpiece on evolution was gloriously feted but at the same time there was growing dissension as to his mechanism of natural selection. Darwin's Pangenesis theory of inheritance, which argued that gemmules within the body reached the sex organs to be passed on to the next generation, had convinced very few. This mechanism was essentially a form of the disproven process of Lamarckian inheritance of acquired characteristics. More importantly, as a form of blending inheritance it would not allow natural selection to operate. In the late nineteenth century, the German evolutionary biologist August Weismann performed an experiment to test Darwin's Pangenesis: he cut off the tails of 68 mice over five generations and found that tail lengths did not differ in subsequent generations, showing that the changes in the body did not affect inheritance. In 1892 he hypothesized the existence of what he called 'germ plasm', the hereditary material that contains the information to form a new body or soma. The effect occurred only one way from the germ plasm to the soma. Although supporting Darwin's natural selection, he had effectively shown Pangenesis must be wrong.

In 1900 two botanical geneticists, the German Carl Correns and the Dutch Hugo de Vries, as well as others separately, rediscovered Mendel's 1865 pea experiments. While experiments had shown particulate inheritance could be consistent with natural selection, this work instead created a schism between those who supported Darwin's natural selection and slow evolution and those such as de Vries who argued that mutational change in inherited characters was the mechanism of rapid evolutionary change. This unresolved issue persisted until the work of statistical geneticists, notably culminating with a 1930 publication, *The Genetical Theory of Natural Selection*, by the British geneticist R. A. Fisher. In this book Fisher showed that continuous variations are the result of discrete genetic differences that Mendel had found and that changes in these genetic variations are driven by Darwin's natural selection. Many other supporting studies followed by field biologists, geneticists and palaeontologists. There is a long list of those who became part of the consortium of people who brought these fields of study together. Prominent among them were the evolutionary biologist Ernst Mayr, the botanist G. Ledyard Stebbins, the population geneticists Theodosius Dobzhansky and J.B.S. Haldane, the ecological geneticist E. B. Ford, the evolutionary ornithologist Bernhard Rensch, the palaeontologist George Gaylord Simpson, as well as others. This reconciliation of Mendel and Darwin was named the 'Modern Synthesis' in 1942 by the English evolutionary biologist Julian Huxley, grandson of Darwin's great supporter T. H. Huxley. Sometimes known as neo-Darwinism, this term unfortunately slights Mendel's essential contributions.

There are also darker legacies attributed to Darwin and although false or mostly false they nevertheless do not disappear. These are the related concepts of social Darwinism and eugenics that have been laid at Darwin's doorstep by those who either do not know his theories or twist them to their own use. Both of these concepts are traceable to the regrettable phrase 'survival of the fittest' proposed by political theorist and philosopher Herbert Spencer. Spencer first used it in 1864 in his *Principles of Biology* after reading *On the Origin of Species*. He tried to draw similarities between his economic theories and the biological theories proposed by Darwin. Under the urging of Wallace, Darwin unfortunately came to use the phrase as synonymous with his 'natural selection'. Darwin did not abandon his natural selection but did oblige Wallace by using Spencer's phrase in the 1869 fifth edition of *On the Origin of Species*. Over the years this has proved an unfortunate alternative because trying to define Spencer's meaning of 'fit' leads to a tautology: who are the survivors? The 'fit' are those that survive. Thus, the phrase becomes 'survival of the survivors'.

Survival of the fittest became closely associated with the theory of social structure titled, misleadingly, 'social Darwinism'. In *The Descent of Man* Darwin discussed natural selection as it applied to humans of his Victorian milieu – with the unquestioned acceptance of the Western world as the pinnacle of civilization, the work strikes us today at best as paternalistic and at worst racist. In this Darwin was much like his contemporaries except that he saw natural selection continuing to affect humans in both savage and civilized societies, but not the societies themselves per se. This was unlike some, such as Wallace, who argued that the effects of natural selection diminished as conscious modern civilized man emerged.

The English essayist William Rathbone Greg agreed with Wallace but argued that all the niceties of civilization, notably medicine and relief for the poor, dampened natural selection's effect on society. Herbert Spencer took it to the obvious conclusion by promoting a laissez-faire approach with no governmental regulation of private businesses and natural selection winnowing out weak elements of society. Darwin muddied the waters by at times seemingly supporting these men's view that supposedly more respectable members of society needed to produce more offspring.

No single, coherent explanation exists to explain the pseudoscience of social Darwinism. One of its better-known iterations argues that the wealth and power of the strong will increase, while that of the weak will decrease – laissez-faire capitalism – hence reference to Spencer's survival of the fittest. Incongruously the concept has also been applied by supporters of governmental socialism and colonization. Whether such societal and economic trends exist in any of these guises is irrelevant because social Darwinism erroneously equates them to the natural world in which variations in organisms are winnowed by natural selection and passed through inheritance to succeeding generations. No such processes operate within human society. Thus, there is a clear disconnect between Darwin's theory of natural selection and social Darwinism, a concept to which Darwin never subscribed but did lean towards.

Survival of the fittest also plays a clear role in the misguided belief that the human species improves by not allowing people deemed inferior to breed, a clear extension of at least one form of social Darwinism. Darwin never advocated such a stratagem, although he certainly suggested that the better-off in society should have more children, which he and Emma put into practice. He believed that all humans form a single species arising from a common ancestor – the theory of monogenism – who he theorized in *The Descent of Man* came from Africa. In the nineteenth century monogenism was strenuously opposed by polygenism, which argued that human races derive from separate origins (sometimes called different species). The latter view contributed to the subjugation of people deemed inferior. Just because monogenists including Darwin argued that humans had a single origin, it did not mean that they were any less prejudiced towards those who belonged to what were deemed to be lesser races or who came from what were seen as inferior countries. As Victorian men they held that their social system was superior to most others and was more likely to triumph in the end. Darwin was raised to believe that slavery was abhorrent but at the same time he held the view that some peoples of the world, such as the Fuegians he met in South America, were primitive savages and a lower grade of human. As he argued in the *Voyage of the HMS Beagle* while railing against slavery, the poorer state of some human beings results from unjust social institutions, not from laws of nature.

A number of threads leading to the origin of eugenics mistakenly tie Darwin to the views of his half-cousin Francis Galton, one of its founders and the man who coined the word 'eugenics' in 1883, the year after Darwin died. The two shared a grandfather, Erasmus, but not a grandmother. An English statistician, Galton read Darwin's work, making the erroneous leap that Darwin's findings could be used to improve the human race, a point with which Darwin disagreed, although he certainly encouraged those who were wealthy and respectable enough to have more children. Some continue to try to read into Darwin's works statements supporting eugenics. These attempts are always out of context. In fact, what Darwin argued is that humans, like all other species, are subject to natural selection, a view we know today to be true but well ahead of its time in the nineteenth century.

The only real connection of Charles Darwin to eugenics was through his son Leonard, his eighth child and the last of the Darwin children to die. Leonard served in the British Army from

1871 starting in the Royal Engineers to his retirement from the service in 1895. He served in various capacities, including several scientific expeditions such as those to observe the transit of Venus in 1874 and 1882. Leonard married twice, first to Elizabeth Frances Fraser and after her death to Charlotte Mildred Massingberd, but there were no children. He helped his sister Henrietta with the proofs of their father's *Expression of the Emotions*. He was also a member of parliament for the Liberal Unionist Party and served as president of the Royal Geographical Society. Leonard took over the helm of the British Eugenics Society in 1911 from its founder Francis Galton, serving in this capacity until 1928. He encouraged the society's members, in an article published in 1916 titled 'Quality Not Quantity', to have more children, but as the movement grew more strident, so did its goals.

In the earlier part of the twentieth century during Leonard Darwin's tenure as president of the society, eugenics found a place in academia. Eugenics societies sprung up in various countries, and international conferences were held. The movement did not remain merely academic following the passage of sterilization laws. One of the earliest and most aggressive adopters was the U.S., which forcibly or without consent sterilized more than 64,000 individuals between 1907 and 1963.[12] Nazi Germany took notice in the 1930s of programmes in the U.S. and soon began their own. Obviously, the Nazi practice of enforced sterilizations of those they deemed inferior was far more insidious and barbaric and went far beyond the schemes of other nations.

Attempts to pull Darwin and his theories into these controversies and abhorrent acts not only sully his reputation, but unequivocally misunderstand and misrepresent his work. Such distortions endure, the most recent being A. N. Wilson's 2017 anti-evolutionary and anti-Darwin screed *Charles Darwin: Victorian Mythmaker*. Wilson writes 'Of these myths, one of the most potent is the Darwinian belief that "all of nature is a constant struggle between power and weakness, a constant struggle of the strong over the weak".' Wilson parenthetically continues in the next paragraph '(The sentence I quoted at the end of the last paragraph was, of course, spoken not by Darwin or Huxley but by Adolf Hitler in a speech entitled "World Jewry and World Markets, the Guilty Men of the World War".)' Attempting to equate contorted Nazi ideology with evolution by means of natural selection beggars belief. The harm is the pretence of it being a biography of Darwin, but, as one reviewer noted, it is simply 'Darwin bashing'. It has even earned a place on a list of the worst books written in the first two decades of this century.[13]

In the final analysis we may ask what sort of person do we believe Charles Robert Darwin was, and how have we come to know so much about this one individual? His quite broad-minded, liberal upbringing shaped his character and political views, including moulding his revulsion to slavery. In another sense he was very much a Victorian man hewing to the conventions of the time, such as woman's place in society. Yet he had many women correspondents with whom he exchanged scientific data and ideas, and also evolving ideas on women's roles. These included Mary Treat, whose interests and expertise lay in botany, entomology and geology; Mary Elizabeth Barber, who made observations on the role of moths in orchid pollination; Dorothy Nevill, who supplied Darwin with plants for his research; the Scottish writer, war correspondent and feminist Florence Caroline Dixie, who wrote to Darwin about travels in South America; and the anti-vivisectionist Frances Power Cobbe. He could have paid closer heed to the writings of his paternal grandfather, Erasmus Darwin, who was a staunch advocate for formal education for women before Charles was born.

Charles and Emma were typical well-to-do upper-class members of English society who made their money through inheritance, business investments and the leasing of land to tenant farmers.

Darwin was a consummate family man, indulging his large brood of children. To most he did not seem arrogant, but rather self-effacing, and scrupulous to a fault in dealing with others. This did not mean he lacked an ego, as he certainly wished the results of his work to be recognized. As with any busy person he did make any number of mistakes for which he tried to atone if he felt he was in the wrong. Darwin held grudges, as witnessed by some of the very early slights he remembered from his youth and young adulthood, probably making him sensitive to the feelings of others. One can speculate that his illnesses, if not caused by, were exacerbated by his sensitivity and aversion to dealing with the public, a trait that intensified with age. Darwin increasingly utilized his cadre of friends and colleagues to champion his ideas, most notably his work on the mutability of species and its cause, natural selection. One could even say he used these people for his purposes in forwarding his ideas. This is very probably true, but these these friends and acquaintainces knew full well what they were doing and why they were doing it. What stands out most about Darwin's intellect was his insatiable curiosity and how he could focus, some might say over-focus, on a topic to tease out the answers to questions that escaped the attention of others. He could be dogged in scientific pursuits. He was extremely hard-working, as witnessed by all he accomplished, even given his repeated debilitating bouts of illnesses. One of his quirkier work habits was to break thick tomes into two or more parts along their spine to create more manageably sized pieces of text with which to work.

Arguably more so than almost any other person who influenced the course of human history, Darwin has been both revered and reviled. This attention spawned an industry around the man and his work, the present biography included. This has not abated over time. If anything, we know more about Darwin now than ever before. Much of this stems from the accessibility and availability of his papers and especially his correspondence. The invention and wider use of the telephone came very late in Darwin's life, but he did receive telegrams from acquaintances by the 1860s, such as from Asa Gray. Yet the single most profound means of correspondence in Victorian England was the Royal Mail, which offered multiple deliveries each day even in areas outside of London, such as where Darwin lived in the village of Downe. This sort of communication was as immediate then as electronic communication is today.

The first publication of Darwin's letters stretches back to 1835 while he was still on the *Beagle*, when his Cambridge mentor John Henslow privately circulated some of his correspondence. His son Francis published more of his letters in 1887. From then on into the twentieth century other volumes of his correspondence have appeared. The pace of publication accelerated greatly when in 1985 the Darwin Correspondence Project began publishing Darwin's letters in chronological order. Twenty-eight volumes exist as of 2021 with two more to come and online versions available for all but the most recent volumes. The project staff calculate that this will eventually include more than 15,000 letters that Darwin exchanged with almost 2,000 correspondents. To this can be added several great boons to all interested parties – online access to many of Darwin's unpublished papers at Cambridge University Library, comprehensive access to many of his works at Darwin Online, and the publication of many of his *Beagle* diaries, field notes and notebooks.

Charles Robert Darwin shares his birthday, 12 February 1809, with another incredible human, Abraham Lincoln, who consistently ranks as either first or second in most polls of the greatest American presidents. Both men had a profound effect on their place and time, Lincoln deeply influencing one nation's identity whereas Darwin fundamentally changed how all humans perceive their place in nature. And his findings still resonate today.

References

Preface

1 Erasmus Darwin, *Zoonomia; or, The Laws of Organic Life*, vol. I, 2nd edn (London, 1796), p. 509.
2 Charles Darwin, *The Autobiography of Charles Darwin, 1809–1882, with the Original Omissions Restored*, ed. Nora Barlow (London, 1958), p. 28.

1 Few Memories of My Mother

1 Charles Darwin, *The Autobiography of Charles Darwin, 1809–1882, with the Original Omissions Restored*, ed. Nora Barlow (London, 1958), p. 45.
2 Ibid., pp. 45–6.
3 Ibid., p. 25.
4 Ibid., p. 28.
5 Ibid., pp. 47–8.

2 Edinburgh Attempt, Cambridge Success

1 Letter from Charles Darwin to his father, 23 October 1825, in *The Correspondence of Charles Darwin*, vol. I: *1821–36*, ed. F. Burkhardt et al. (Cambridge, 1985), pp. 18–19.
2 Charles Darwin, *The Autobiography of Charles Darwin, 1809–1882, with the Original Omissions Restored*, ed. Nora Barlow (London, 1958), p. 47.
3 Richard Broke Freeman, 'Darwin's Negro Bird-stuffer', *Notes and Records of the Royal Society of London*, XXXIII (1978–9), pp. 83–6.

4   Letter from Charles Darwin to his sister Susan, 29 January 1826, in *The Correspondence of Charles Darwin*, vol. I, p. 29.

5   Letter from Charles Darwin to Joseph Dalton Hooker, 29 May 1854, in *The Correspondence of Charles Darwin*, vol. V: *1851–55*, ed. F. Burkhardt et al. (Cambridge, 1989), p. 195.

6   Darwin, *Autobiography*, p. 53.

7   Ibid.

8   Ibid., pp. 50–51.

9   Ibid., pp. 53–4.

10 Ibid., p. 59.

11 Ibid.

12 'Se non è vero, è molto ben trovato' (If it is not true, it is very well invented). *De gli heroici furori* [1585] (*The Heroic Furies*; also translated as *On Heroic Frenzies*), as quoted in *A Book of Quotations, Proverbs and Household Words*, ed. Sir William Gurney Benham (Philadelphia, PA, 1907). Variant translations: If it is not true, it is well conceived; If it is not true, it is a good story.

13 Ibid., p. 62.

14 Ibid., p. 69.

15 Darwin, *Autobiography*, p. 72.

3 The Most Important Event in My Life

1   Charles Darwin, *The Autobiography of Charles Darwin, 1809–1882, with the Original Omissions Restored*, ed. Nora Barlow (London, 1958), p. 76.

2   Letter from Charles Darwin to John Henslow, 30 October 1831, in *The Correspondence of Charles Darwin*, vol. I: *1821–36*, ed. F. Burkhardt et al. (Cambridge, 1985), p. 176.

3   In *Journal and Remarks* Darwin mentioned Humboldt on 35 occasions and Lyell 24 times. Charles Darwin, *Journal and Remarks, 1832–1836*, vol. III: *Narrative of the Surveying Voyages of His Majesty's Ships Adventure and Beagle, between the Years 1826 and 1836, Describing Their*

Examination of the Southern Shores of South America and the Beagle's Circumnavigation of the Globe (London, 1839).

4 Letter from Emily Catherine Darwin to Charles, 8 January–4 February 1832, in *The Correspondence of Charles Darwin*, vol. I, pp. 192–3; letter from Fanny Owen to Charles, 1 March 1832, ibid., pp. 213–15.

5 Darwin, *Autobiography*, pp. 73–5.

6 Letter from Charles Darwin to John S. Henslow, 18 May–16 June 1832, in *The Correspondence of Charles Darwin*, vol. I, p. 238.

7 Letter from Charles Darwin to John M. Herbert, 2 June 1833, ibid., p. 320.

8 Letter from Susan Darwin to Charles Darwin, 15 October 1833, ibid., pp. 337–8.

9 Letter from John S. Henslow to Charles Darwin, 15–21 January 1833, ibid., pp. 292–64. Darwin's letter to Henslow from Valparaiso, 24 July 1834, ibid., pp. 397–402, mentions two letters Darwin received from Henslow, one dated 12 December 1833 and the other 15 January 1833. Only the latter letter is known.

10 Letter from Charles Darwin to Susan Darwin, 19 July–12 August 1835, ibid., pp. 457–9.

11 Darwin, *Journal and Remarks*, p. 526.

12 The sense of Herschel's 'mystery of mysteries' has been published in various places. One version is in a letter from Charles Lyell to William Whewell. 'You remember what Herschel said in his letter to me. If I had stated as plainly as he has done the possibility of the introduction or origination of fresh species being a natural, in contradistinction to a miraculous process, I should have raised a host of prejudices against me, which are unfortunately opposed at every step to any philosopher who attempts to address the public on these mysterious subjects.' Charles Darwin, *The Life and Letters of Charles Darwin, Including an Autobiographical Chapter*, 3 vols, ed. Francis Darwin (1887), vol. II, p. 191.

4 A New Scientific Career and a New Wife

1 Charles Darwin, 'Darwin's Notes on Transmutation of Species. Part I. First Notebook [B] (July 1837–February 1838)', ed. Gavin de Beer, *Bulletin of the British Museum (Natural History)*, II/2 (1960), pp. 45–6.

2 Charles Darwin, 'Darwin's Ornithological Notes', ed. Nora Barlow, *Bulletin of the British Museum (Natural History)*, II/7 (1963), p. 262.

3 John Gould, 'On a New Rhea (*Rhea Darwinii*) from Mr Darwin's Collection', *Proceedings of the Zoological Society of London*, V/51 (1837), pp. 35–6; Charles Darwin, 'Remarks on the Habits of the Genera *Geospiza, Camarhynchus, Cactornis* and *Certheidea* of Gould', *Proceedings of the Zoological Society of London*, V/53 (1837), p. 49.

4 Charles Darwin, 'Notes on Marriage', July 1839, in *The Correspondence of Charles Darwin*, vol. II: *1837–43*, ed. F. Burkhardt et al. (Cambridge, 1985), p. 444.

5 A Momentous Move

1 Letter from Charles Darwin to his sister Catherine, 24 July 1842, in *The Correspondence of Charles Darwin*, vol. I I: *1837–43*, ed. F. Burkhardt et al. (Cambridge, 1986), pp. 323–5.

2 Gwen Raverat, *Period Piece: A Cambridge Childhood* (London, 1974), pp. 157–8.

3 Hedley Atkins, *Down House, the Home of the Darwins: Story of a House and the People Who Lived There* (London, 1974), pp. 106–25.

4 'Down House during the War', *Advancement of Science*, III/11 (1945), pp. 280–81.

5 Charles Darwin, *The Autobiography of Charles Darwin, 1809–1882, with the Original Omissions Restored*, ed. Nora Barlow (London, 1958), p. 107.

6 Letter from Charles Darwin to J. D. Hooker, 7 January 1845, in *The Correspondence of Charles Darwin*, vol. III: *1844–46*, ed. F. Burkhardt et al. (Cambridge, 1987), p. 108.

7 Letter from J. D. Hooker to Charles Darwin, 14 September 1845, ibid.,
   p. 254.

6 Where Does He Do His Barnacles?

1 Letter from John M. Herbert to Charles Darwin, early May 1831, in *The
   Correspondence of Charles Darwin*, vol. I: *1821–36*, ed. F. Burkhardt et al.
   (Cambridge, 1985), pp. 122–3.
2 Letter from Emily Catherine Darwin to Charles Darwin, 13 November
   1848, in *The Correspondence of Charles Darwin*, vol. IV: *1847–50*,
   ed. F. Burkhardt et al. (Cambridge, 1988), pp. 182–3.
3 Letter from Charles Darwin to William Darwin Fox, 24 October
   1852, in *The Correspondence of Charles Darwin*, vol. V: *1851–55*,
   ed. F. Burkhardt et al. (Cambridge, 1989), p. 100.

7 Lyell's Words Come True with a Vengeance

1 Letter from Charles Darwin to Charles Lyell, 14 September 1838, in *The
   Correspondence of Charles Darwin*, vol. II: *1837–43*, ed. F. Burkhardt et al.
   (Cambridge, 1985), pp. 103–7.
2 In a letter to Joseph Hooker, 8 February 1847, Darwin wrote, 'I hardly
   know when I shall come to Kew for a morning to hear what you have
   to say about my species-sketch.' Footnote 5 for the letter indicates
   that Hooker probably received a fair copy of the essay of 1844 on his
   visit to Down House. This may have been on 16 January 1847. See *The
   Correspondence of Charles Darwin*, vol. V: *1851–55*, ed. F. Burkhardt et al.
   (Cambridge, 1989), p. 11.
3 Letter from Charles Darwin to Asa Gray, 5 September 1857, in *The
   Correspondence of Charles Darwin*, vol. VI: *1856–57*, ed. F. Burkhardt et
   al. (Cambridge, 1990), pp. 445–50.
4 Thomas Henry Huxley, 'Lectures on General Natural History. Lecture
   XII: The Cirripedia', *Medical Times and Gazette*, n.s. XV (1857),
   pp. 238–41.
5 Letter from Charles Lyell to Charles Darwin, 1–2 May 1856, in
   The Correspondence of Charles Darwin, vol. VI, pp. 89–92.

6 Both letter and essay manuscript sent by Wallace to Darwin have not
   been located, although the essay was published in 1858. Opinions vary
   but the letter and manuscript were probably posted between 5 and 19
   March 1858 and probably arrived at Down House in early June.

7 Charles Lyell probably first recommended Wallace's 1855 paper on
   a visit to Down House in 1856. Letter and manuscript from Charles
   Darwin to Charles Lyell, 18 June 1858, in *The Correspondence of Charles
   Darwin*, vol. VII: *1858–59*, ed. F. Burkhardt et al. (Cambridge, 1991),
   footnote 2, p. 107; Edward Blyth had also written to Darwin about
   Wallace's paper on 5 December 1855: see *The Correspondence of Charles
   Darwin*, vol. V, ed., F. Burkhardt et al. (Cambridge, 1989), pp. 519–22.

8 Letter from Charles Darwin to Alfred Russel Wallace, 22 December
   1857, *Correspondence*, vol. VI, pp. 514–15.

9 Letter and manuscript from Charles Darwin to Charles Lyell, 18 June
   1858, in *Correspondence*, vol. VII, pp. 107–8.

10 Letter from Charles Darwin to Charles Lyell, 25 June 1858, ibid.,
   p. 118, footnote 2 indicates that Lyell may have written a letter to Alfred
   Russel Wallace about Wallace's manuscript and sent it to Darwin, to be
   forwarded to Wallace. The letter has not been found.

11 Letter from Charles Darwin to J. D. Hooker, 29 June 1858, ibid.,
   pp. 121–2.

12 Letter and manuscript from Charles Darwin to John Murray,
   3 November 1859, in *Correspondence*, vol. VII,
   pp. 365–6.

13 Charles Darwin, *On the Origin of Species by Means of Natural Selection,
   or the Preservation of Favoured Races in the Struggle for Life*, 1st edn
   (London, 1859), p. 490.

14 Charles Darwin, *On the Origin of Species by Means of Natural Selection,
   or the Preservation of Favoured Races in the Struggle for Life*, 2nd edn
   (London, 1860), p. 490.

15 Letter from Charles Darwin to J. D. Hooker, 29 March 1863, in
   The Correspondence of Charles Darwin, vol. XII: *1864*, ed. F. Burkhardt et
   al. (Cambridge, 1999), p. 278.

16 Letter from Charles Darwin to Baden Powell, 18 January 1860, in *The
   Correspondence of Charles Darwin*, vol. VIII: *1860*, ed. F. Burkhardt et al.
   (Cambridge, 1993), pp. 39–40.

17 Letter written by Charles Darwin to the *Gardener's Chronicle*, 13 April 1860, in *Correspondence*, vol. VIII, p. 156.

8 Reviews and Reactions

1 Anonymous, 'Charles Darwin on the Origin of Species', *Chambers's Journal of Popular Literature, Science and Arts*, XI (1859), pp. 388–91.

2 Anonymous, '[Review of] On the Origin of Species', *Saturday Review*, VIII (1859), pp. 775–6.

3 Anonymous, 'Review of the Origin of Species', *John Bull and Britannia*, XXXIX/2,037 (1859), p. 11.

4 Letter from Charles Darwin to Asa Gray, 5 June 1861, in *The Correspondence of Charles Darwin*, vol. IX: *1861*, ed. F. Burkhardt et al. (Cambridge, 1994), p. 163.

5 Letter from Charles Darwin to Asa Gray, 19 January 1863, in *The Correspondence of Charles Darwin*, vol. XI: *1863*, ed. F. Burkhardt et al. (Cambridge, 1991), p. 57. Letter from Asa Gray to Charles Darwin, 24 July 1865, in *The Correspondence of Charles Darwin*, vol. XIII: *1865*, ed. F. Burkhardt et al. (Cambridge, 1991), p. 208.

6 Charles Kingsley, *The Water-Babies: A Fairy Tale for a Land Baby* (London, 1863), p. 153.

7 [Richard, Owen], 'Review of *Origin* & Other Works', *Edinburgh Review*, CXI (1860), pp. 487–532; [Samuel Wilberforce], '[Review of] On the Origin of Species, by Means of Natural Selection; or the Preservation of Favoured Races in the Struggle for Life', *Quarterly Review*, CVIII (1860), pp. 225–64.

8 Charles Darwin, *On the Origin of Species by Means of Natural Selection, or the Preservation of Favoured Races in the Struggle for Life*, 1st edn (London, 1859), p. 184.

9 Ibid., p. 310.

10 Letter from Charles Darwin to Charles Lyell, 10 December 1859, in *The Correspondence of Charles Darwin*, vol. VII: *1858–59*, ed. F. Burkhardt et al. (Cambridge, 1991), pp. 421–4.

11 Anonymous, '[Review of] On the Origin of Species', *Saturday Review*, pp. 775–6.

12 William Thomson, 'On the Secular Cooling of the Earth', *Transactions of the Royal Society of Edinburgh*, XXIII (1862), pp. 167–9.

13 Richard Owen, On the *Archeopteryx* of von Mayer, with a Description of the Fossil Remains of a Long-tailed species, from the Lithographic Stone of Solenhofen', *Philosophical Transactions of the Royal Society of London*, CLIII (1863), pp. 33–47.

14 John William Dawson, 'On the Structure of Certain Organic Remains in the Laurentian Limestones of Canada', *Quarterly Journal of the Geological Society*, XXI (1864), pp. 51–9.

15 Charles Darwin, *On the Origin of Species by Means of Natural Selection, or the Preservation of Favoured Races in the Struggle for Life*, 4th edn (London, 1866), p. 371.

16 Charles Darwin, *On the Origin of Species by Means of Natural Selection, or the Preservation of Favoured Races in the Struggle for Life*, 6th edn (London, 1872), p. 287.

17 [Fleeming Jenkin], '[Review of] *The Origin of Species*', *North British Review*, XLVI (June 1867), pp. 277–318.

18 Gregor Mendel, 'Versuche über Pflanzenhybriden', *Verhandlungen des naturforschenden Vereines in Brünn*, IV (1866), pp. 3–47.

19 St George Jackson Mivart, 'Contributions towards a More Complete Knowledge of the Axial Skeleton in the Primates', *Proceedings of the Zoological Society of London*, XXXIII (1865), pp. 545–92; 'On the Appendicular Skeleton of the Primates', *Philosophical Transactions of the Royal Society of London*, CLVII (1867), pp. 294–429.

20 St George Jackson Mivart, *On the Genesis of Species* (London, 1871).

21 Charles Darwin, *On the Origin of Species*, 6th edn, pp. 151–2.

22 St George Jackson Mivart, '[Review of] *The Descent of Man*, and Selection in Relation to Sex', *Quarterly Review*, CXXXIII (July 1871), pp. 47–90.

23 Letter from Charles Darwin to Alfred R. Wallace, 12 July 1871, in *The Correspondence of Charles Darwin*, vol. XIX: *1871*, ed. F. Burkhardt et al. (Cambridge, 2012), pp. 485–6.

24 Herbert Spencer, *The Principles of Biology*, vol. I (London, 1864), p. 290.

25 Henry Fawcett, 'A Popular Exposition of Mr Darwin on the Origin of Species', *Macmillan's Magazine*, III (December 1860), p. 81; John S. Henslow, 'Letter from Professor Henslow', *Macmillian's Magazine*, III (January 1861), p. 336.

9 Bringing the 'Big Book' to Fruition

1 Charles Darwin, 'On the Three Remarkable Sexual Forms of *Catasetum tridentatum*, an Orchid in the Possession of the Linnean Society', *Proceedings of the Linnean Society of London*: Botany, VI/2 (1862), pp. 151–7.

2 Letter from J. D. Hooker to Charles Darwin, 13 May 1866, in *The Correspondence of Charles Darwin*, vol. XIV: *1866*, ed. F. Burkhardt et al. (Cambridge, 2004), p. 171.

3 Charles Darwin, *The Life and Letters of Charles Darwin, Including an Autobiographical Chapter*, 3 vols, ed. Francis Darwin (1887), vol. III, p. 274.

4 [George Douglas Campbell], 'The Supernatural', *Edinburgh Review*, CXVI (1862), pp. 589–90.

5 Letter from T. H. Huxley to Charles Darwin, 16 July 1865, in *The Correspondence of Charles Darwin*, vol. XIII: *1865*, ed. F. Burkhardt et al. (Cambridge, 2002), p. 203.

6 Letter from Charles Darwin to Alfred Russel Wallace, 6 February 1866, in *Correspondence*, vol. XIV, pp. 44–5. The following quote from the letter has been used to suggest that Darwin was thinking about particulate or non-blending inheritance. 'I do not think you understand what I mean by the non-blending of certain varieties. It does not refer to fertility; an instance will explain; I crossed the Painted Lady & Purple sweet-peas, which are very differently coloured vars, & got, even out of the same pod, both varieties perfect but none intermediate. Something of this kind I should think must occur at first with your butterflies & the 3 forms of Lythrum; tho' these cases are in appearance so wonderful, I do not know that they are really more so than every female in the world producing *distinct* male & female offspring.' Although tantalizing, Darwin never followed through on the significance of this experiment.

7 Commentary by Henrietta (Darwin) Litchfield on meeting Tennyson, in *Emma Darwin: A Century of Family Letters, 1792–1896*, 2 vols, ed. H. E. Litchfield (London, 1904), vol. II, pp. 220–21.

8 Letter from Charles Darwin to Marian Evans (George Eliot), 30 March 1873, in *The Correspondence of Charles Darwin*, vol. XXI: *1873*, ed. F. Burkhardt et al. (Cambridge, 2002), p. 144.

9 [George Henry Lewes], '[Review of] 'Darwin on Domestication and Variation', *Pall Mall Gazette*, VII (1868), pp. 555, 636–7, 652.

10 J. David Archibald, *Aristotle's Ladder, Darwin's Tree: The Evolution of Visual Metaphors for Biological Order* (New York, 2017), pp. 108–12.

11 Raman Akinyanju Lawal et al., 'The Wild Species Genome Ancestry of Domestic Chickens', *BMC Biology*, XVIII/13 (2020), bmcbiol. biomecentral.com.

12 Letter from Charles Darwin to Asa Gray, 3 April 1860, in *The Correspondence of Charles Darwin*, vol. VIII: *1860*, ed. F. Burkhardt et al. (Cambridge, 1993), p. 140.

10 Teasing Plants and Tending Worms

1 Letter from Charles Darwin to E. R. Lankester, 22 March 1871, in *The Correspondence of Charles Darwin*, vol. XIX: *1871*, ed. F. Burkhardt et al. (Cambridge, 2012), p. 205.

2 Charles Darwin's testimony given to the commission in *Report of the Royal Commission on the Practice of Subjecting Live Animals to Experiments for Scientific Purposes; with the Minutes of Evidence and Appendix* (London, 1876), p. 233.

3 Letter from Emma Darwin to her daughter-in-law Sara, in *Emma Darwin: A Century of Family Letters, 1792–1896*, 2 vols, ed. H. E. Litchfield (London, 1904), vol. II, pp. 320–21.

4 'On the Formation of Mould', *Proceedings of the Geological Society of London*, II (1838), pp. 574–6.

5 Charles Darwin, *On the Origin of Species by Means of Natural Selection, or the Preservation of Favoured Races in the Struggle for Life*, 1st edn (London, 1859), pp. 73–4.

11 Not the Least Afraid of Death

1 Notes written by Emma Darwin shortly before Charles Darwin's death, in *Emma Darwin: A Century of Family Letters, 1792–1896*, 2 vols, ed. H. E. Litchfield (London, 1904), vol. II, p. 329.

2 Elizabeth Cotton (Lady Hope), 'Darwin and Christianity', *Watchman-Examiner*, new series, 3 (19 August 1915), p. 1071.

3 Letter from Francis Darwin possibly to A. Le Lievre, 27 November 1917, reprinted in James Moore, *The Darwin Legend* (London, 1995), p. 145; 'Charles Darwin's Death-bed: Story of Conversion Denied', *The Christian*, 23 February 1922, p. 12.

4 Charles Darwin, *The Autobiography of Charles Darwin, 1809–1882, with the Original Omissions Restored*, ed. Nora Barlow (London, 1958), p. 57.

5 Alfred, Lord Tennyson, *In Memoriam A.H.H.* (London, 1850), p. 60.

6 Letter from Charles Darwin to Asa Gray, 22 May 1860, *The Correspondence of Charles Darwin*, vol. VIII, ed. F. Burkhardt et al. (Cambridge, 1993), p. 224.

7 Letter from Charles Darwin to Frederick McDermott, 24 May 1880, Darwin Correspondence Project, 'Letter no. 12851', available at www.darwinproject.ac.uk.

8 Malcolm Brown, 'Good Religions Needs Good Science', www.cofe.anglican.org, 16 September 2008.

9 James R. Moore, 'Charles Darwin Lies in Westminster Abbey', *Biological Journal of the Linnean Society*, XVII (1982), pp. 97–113.

10 J. David Archibald, *Charles Darwin: A Reference Guide to His Life and Works* (Lanham, MD, 2019), p. 6.

11 Arthur Holmes, 'Radium and the Evolution of the Earth's Crust', *Nature*, XCI (1913), p. 398.

12 Paul A. Lombardo, *Three Generations, No Imbeciles: Eugenics, the Supreme Court, and Buck v. Bell* (Boulder, 2008).

13 A. N. Wilson, *Charles Darwin: Victorian Mythmaker* (London, 2017), p. 362; Joanny Moulin, '"Darwin Bashing": Review of A. N. Wilson's "Charles Darwin, Victorian Mythmaker"', *Biography Society* (13 November 2017), www.biographysociety.org; Wikipedia, 'List of Books Considered the Worst', www.en.wikipedia.org.

Bibliography

Archibald, J. David, *Origins of Darwin's Evolution: Solving the Species Puzzle through Time and Place* (New York, 2017)

Ashworth, J. H., 'Charles Darwin as a Student in Edinburgh, 1825–1827', *Proceedings of the Royal Society of Edinburgh*, LV/10, part II (1935)

Beck, Richard, *A Treatise on the Construction, Proper Use, and Capabilities of the Smith, Beck, and Beck's Achromatic Microscopes* (London, 1865)

Bell, T., *Reptilia, Part 5 of The Zoology of the Voyage of HMS Beagle, under the Command of Captain FitzRoy, R.N., during the Years 1832 to 1863,* ed. C. R. Darwin (London, 1843)

Berra, Tim M., *Darwin and His Children: His Other Legacy* (Oxford, 2013)

Browne, Janet, *Charles Darwin: A Biography*, vol. I: *Voyaging* (New York, 1995)

—, *Charles Darwin: A Biography*, vol. II: *The Power of Place* (New York, 2002)

Burchfield, Joe D., 'Darwin and the Dilemma of Geological Time', *Isis*, 65 (1974)

[Butler, Samuel], *Erewhon; or, Over the Range* (London, 1872)

—, *Evolution, Old and New; or, The Theories of Buffon, Dr Erasmus Darwin, and Lamarck, as Compared with that of Mr Charles Darwin* (London, 1879)

Carpenter, Humphrey, *The Seven Lives of John Murray: The Story of a Publishing Dynasty* (London, 2008)

[Chambers, Robert], *Vestiges of the Natural History of Creation* (London, 1844)

Colp, Ralph, *To Be an Invalid: The Illness of Charles Darwin* (Chicago, IL, 1977)

—, *Darwin's Illness* (Gainesville, FL, 2008)

Correns, Carl, 'G. Mendel's Regel über das Verhalten der Nachkommenschaft der Rassenbastarde', *Berichte der Deutschen Botanischen Gesellschaft*, XVIII (1900)

Costa, James T., *Wallace, Darwin, and the Origin of Species* (Cambridge, MA, 2014)

Darwin, Charles R., *Extracts from Letters Addressed to Professor Henslow* (Cambridge, 1835)

—, *Journal of Researches into the Natural History and Geology of the Countries Visited during the Voyage of HMS 'Beagle' round the World* (London, 1839)

—, 'Observations on the Parallel Roads of Glen Roy, and of Other Parts of Lochaber in Scotland, with an Attempt to Prove That They Are of Marine Origin', *Philosophical Transactions of the Royal Society*, CXXIX (1839)

—, *Questions about the Breeding of Animals* (London, 1839)

—, *The Structure and Distribution of Coral Reefs: Being the First Part of the Geology of the Voyage of the 'Beagle', under the Command of Capt. FitzRoy, R.N. during the Years 1832 to 1836* (London, 1842)

—, *Geological Observations on the Volcanic Islands Visited during the Voyage of HMS 'Beagle', Together with Some Brief Notices of the Geology of Australia and the Cape of Good Hope: Being the Second Part of the Geology of the Voyage of the 'Beagle', under the Command of Capt. FitzRoy, R.N. during the Years 1832 to 1836* (London, 1844)

—, *Journal of Researches into the Natural History and Geology of the Countries Visited during the Voyage of HMS 'Beagle' round the World*, 2nd edn (London, 1845)

—, *Geological Observations on South America: Being the Third Part of the Geology of the Voyage of the 'Beagle', under the Command of Capt. FitzRoy, R.N. during the Years 1832 to 1836* (London, 1846)

—, *A Monograph on the Fossil Lepadidae; or, Pedunculated Cirripedes of Great Britain*, vol. I (London, 1851)

—, *A Monograph of the Sub-class Cirripedia, with Figures of All the Species*, vol. I: *The Lepadidae; or, Pedunculated Cirripedes* (London, 1851)

—, *A Monograph of the Sub-class Cirripedia, with Figures of All the Species*, vol. II: *The Balanidae (or Sessile Cirripedes); the Verrucidae* (London, 1854)

—, *A Monograph on the Fossil Balanidae and Verrucidae of Great Britain*, vol. II (London, 1854)

—, *On the Origin of Species by Means of Natural Selection, or the Preservation of Favoured Races in the Struggle for Life*, 3rd edn (London, 1861)

—, *On the Various Contrivances by Which British and Foreign Orchids Are Fertilised by Insects* (London, 1862)

—, 'On the Movements and Habits of Climbing Plants', *Journal of the Linnean Society of London*: Botany, IX (1865)

—, *Queries about Expression* (Down House, 1867)

—, *The Variation of Animals and Plants under Domestication*, 2 vols (London, 1868)

—, *On the Origin of Species by Means of Natural Selection, or the Preservation of Favoured Races in the Struggle for Life*, 5th edn (London, 1869)

—, *The Descent of Man, and Selection in Relation to Sex*, 2 vols (London, 1871)

—, *The Expression of the Emotions in Man and Animals* (London, 1872)

—, *Insectivorous Plants* (London, 1875)

—, *The Movements and Habits of Climbing Plants*, 2nd edn (London, 1875)

—, *The Effects of Cross and Self Fertilisation in the Vegetable Kingdom* (London, 1876)

—, 'A Biographical Sketch of an Infant', *Mind: A Quarterly Review of Psychology and Philosophy*, II/7 (July 1877)

—, *The Different Forms of Flowers on Plants of the Same Species* (London, 1877)

—, 'Preliminary Notice', in Ernst Krause, *Erasmus Darwin* (London, 1879)

—, *The Power of Movement in Plants* (London, 1880)

—, *The Formation of Vegetable Mould, through the Action of Worms, with Observations on Their Habits* (London, 1881)

—, *The Foundations of the Origin of Species: Two Essays Written in 1842 and 1844* (Cambridge, 1909)

—, 'Darwin's Notebooks on Transmutation of Species. Part II. Second Notebook [C] (February–July 1838)', *Bulletin of the British Museum (Natural History)*, II/3 (1960)

—, 'Darwin's Notebooks on Transmutation of Species. Part III. Third Notebook [D] (15 July–2 October 1838)', *Bulletin of the British Museum (Natural History)*, II/4 (1960)

—, 'Darwin's Notebooks on Transmutation of Species. Part IV. Fourth Notebook [E] (October 1838–10 July 1839)', *Bulletin of the British Museum (Natural History)*, II/5 (1960)

—, 'Darwin's Notebooks on Transmutation of Species Addenda and Corrigenda', *Bulletin of the British Museum (Natural History)*, II/6 (1961)

—, 'Darwin's Notebooks on Transmutation of Species, Part VI. Pages Excised by Darwin', *Bulletin of the British Museum (Natural History)*, III/5 (1967)

—, *Charles Darwin's Natural Selection: Being the Second Part of His Big Species Book Written from 1856 to 1858*, ed. R. C. Stauffer (Cambridge, 1975)

—, 'Darwin's Notebooks on Transmutation of Species, The Red Notebook of Charles Darwin', *Bulletin of the British Museum (Natural History)*, 7 (1980)

—, *The Correspondence of Charles Darwin*, ed. F. Burkhardt et al., vols I–XXVII, *1821–79* (Cambridge, 1985–2019)

—, and Alfred Russel Wallace, 'On the Tendency of Species to Form Varieties; and on the Perpetuation of Varieties and Species by Natural Means of Selection', *Journal of the Proceedings of the Linnean Society of London: Zoology*, III (20 August 1858)

Darwin, Erasmus, *Zoonomia; or, The Laws of Organic Life*, 3 parts (London, 1794–6)

—, *The Temple of Nature; or, The Origin of Society* (London, 1803)

Darwin, Leonard, 'Quality Not Quantity', *Eugenics Review*, II (1916)

Desmond, Adrian, and James Moore, *Darwin* (London, 1991)

de Vries, Hugo, *Die Mutationstheorie, Versuche und Beobachtungen über die Entstehung von Arten im Pflanzenreich* (Leipzig, 1901–3)

Eliot, George, *Adam Bede* (Edinburgh, 1859)

—, *Mill on the Floss* (Edinburgh, 1860)

—, *Silas Marner* (Edinburgh, 1861)

Freeman, Richard Broke, *Charles Darwin: A Companion* (Folkestone, Kent, 1978)

—, *The Works of Charles Darwin: An Annotated Bibliographical Handlist*, 2nd edn (Folkestone, Kent, 1978)

Galton, Francis, *Inquiries into Human Faculty and Its Development* (London, 1883)

Gould, John, 'On a New Rhea (*Rhea Darwinii*) from Mr Darwin's Collection', *Proceedings of the Zoological Society of London*, V/51 (1837)

—, *Birds, Part 3 of The Zoology of the Voyage of HMS 'Beagle', under the Command of Captain FitzRoy, R.N., during the Years 1832 to 1836*, ed. C. R. Darwin (London, 1841)

Grant, Robert E., 'Notice Regarding the Ova of the *Pontobdella muricata*, Lam.', *Edinburgh Journal of Science*, VII/1 (Edinburgh, 1827)

[Gray, Asa], 'Review of Darwin's Theory on the Origin of Species by Means of Natural Selection', *American Journal of Science and Arts*, XXIX (1860)

—, '[Review of] On the Origin of Species', *Atlantic Monthly*, VI (1860)

Greg, William Rathbone, 'On the Failure of "Natural Selection" in the Case of Man', *Fraser's Magazine* (September 1868)

Henslow, John Stevens, 'Letter from Professor Henslow', *Macmillian's Magazine*, III (1861)

Herbert, Sandra, *Charles Darwin, Geologist* (Ithaca, NY, 2005)

Hooker, Joseph D., 'An Enumeration of the Plants of the Galapagos Archipelago; with Descriptions of Those Which Are New', *Transactions of the Linnean Society of London*, XX (1844, 1847, 1851)

—, 'On the Vegetation of the Galapagos Archipelago, as Compared with That of Some Other Tropical Islands and of the Continent of America', *Transactions of the Linnean Society of London*, XX (1847, 1851)

Huxley, Julian, *Evolution: The Modern Synthesis* (London, 1942)

Huxley, Thomas Henry, *Evidence as to Man's Place in Nature (London, 1863)*

Jenyns, L., *Fish, Part 4 of The Zoology of the Voyage of HMS 'Beagle', under the Command of Captain FitzRoy, R.N., during the Years 1832 to 1836*, ed. C. R. Darwin (London, 1842)

Johnson, Curtis N., *Darwin's Historical Sketch: An Examination of the 'Preface' to the Origin of Species* (Oxford, 2019)

Keynes, Randal, *Annie's Box: Charles Darwin, His Daughter and Human Evolution* (London, 2001)

Krause, Ernst, 'Zeitschrift Fur Einheitliche Weltanschauung Aufgrund Der Entwicklungslehre', *Kosmos*, vol. VI (October 1879)

Lyell, Charles, *Principles of Geology*, 2 vols, 1st edn (London, 1830, 1832, 1833)

—, *The Geological Evidences of the Antiquity of Man, with Remarks on Theories on the Origin of Species by Variations* (London, 1863)

—, *Principles of Geology*, 2 vols, 10th edn (London, 1866–8)

MacGillivray, William, *A History of British Birds, Indigenous and Migratory*, 5 vols (London, 1837–52)

[Malthus, Thomas Robert], *An Essay on the Principle of Population, as It Affects the Future Improvement of Society with Remarks on the Speculations of Mr. Godwin, M. Condorcet, and Other Writers* (London, 1798)

Matthew, Patrick, *Naval Timber and Arboriculture* (Edinburgh, 1831)

Milner, Richard, *Darwin's Universe: Evolution from A to Z* (Oakland, CA, 2009)

Owen, R., *Fossil Mammalia, Part 1 of The Zoology of the Voyage of HMS 'Beagle', under the Command of Captain FitzRoy, R.N., during the Years 1832 to 1836*, ed. C. R. Darwin (London, 1840)

—, 'Review of *Origin* & Other Works', *Edinburgh Review*, CXI (1860)

Paley, William, *The Principles of Moral and Political Philosophy* (London, 1785)

—, *Natural Theology or Evidences of the Existence and Attributes of the Deity* (London, 1802)

Petre, Jonathan, 'Church Makes "Ludicrous" Apology to Charles Darwin – 126 Years after His Death', *Daily Mail* (13 September 2008)

Richards, Robert J., *Was Hitler a Darwinian? Disputed Questions in the History of Evolutionary Theory* (Chicago, IL, 2013)

Rolle, Friedrich, 'Der Archaeopteryx oder Urvogel der Jura-Zeit', *Hertha*, I (1867)

Stephens, James F., *Illustrations of British Entomology* (London, 1829–32)

Stott, Rebecca, *Darwin and the Barnacle: The Story of One Tiny Creature and History's Most Spectacular Scientific Breakthrough* (London, 2003)

Thomson, Keith, *HMS Beagle: The Story of Darwin's Ship* (New York, 1995)

Uglow, Jenny, *The Lunar Men: Five Friends Whose Curiosity Changed the World* (New York, 2002)

von Meyer, H. '*Archaeopterix lithographica* (Vogel-Feder) und *Pterodactylus* von Solenhofen', *Neues Jahrbuch für Geologie und Paläontologie/Monatshefte* (1861)

Wallace, Alfred Russel, 'On the Law Which Has Regulated the Introduction of New Species', *Annals and Magazine of Natural History* II Series (1855)

—, *The Malay Archipelago* (London, 1869)

—, *Darwinism: An Exposition of the Theory of Natural Selection, with Some of Its Applications* (London, 1889)

Waterhouse, G. R., *Mammalia, Part 2 of The Zoology of the Voyage of HMS Beagle, under the Command of Captain FitzRoy, R.N., during the Years 1832 to 1836*, ed. C. R. Darwin (London, 1839)

—, 'Descriptions of Coleopterous Insects Collected by Charles Darwin, Esq., in the Galapagos Islands', *Annals and Magazine of Natural History, including Zoology, Botany, and Geology*, XVI (1845)

Wedgwood, Barbara, and Hensleigh Wedgwood, *The Wedgwood Circle, 1730–1897: Four Generations of a Family and Their Friends* (London, 1980)

Westbury, Michael, et al., 'A Mitogenomic Timetree for Darwin's Enigmatic South American Mammal *Macrauchenia patachonica*', *Nature Communications*, VIII (2017)

White, Gilbert, *The Natural History and Antiquities of Selborne* (London, 1789)

[Wilberforce, S.], '[Review of] On the Origin of Species, by Means of Natural Selection; or the Preservation of Favoured Races in the Struggle for Life', *Quarterly Review*, CVIII (1860)

Wyhe, John van, *Charles Darwin in Cambridge: The Most Joyful Years* (Singapore, 2014)

—, *The Complete Work of Charles Darwin Online*, http://darwin-online.org. uk, 2006–present

Acknowledgements

The author thanks John van Wyhe for suggesting to Reaktion Books
that I write this short biography of Charles Robert Darwin for their
Critical Lives Series. My good friends and colleagues Annalisa Berta and
Roger Sabbadini graciously read and commented on a later version of the
manuscript, for which I am very thankful. My wife and best friend Gloria
Bader patiently read several versions of the manuscript, which was no
doubt a labour of love.

I thank the editors and staff of Reaktion Books for help in bringing this
project to fruition.

A number of online sources proved immensely helpful: the Biodiversity
Heritage Library, the Darwin Correspondence Project and Darwin Online.
I thank San Diego State University Interlibrary Loan for obtaining copies
or originals of materials used in this book. The Bibliography gives sources
that could not be included in the References or main text because of space
constraints and are here gratefully acknowledged.

Photo Acknowledgements

The author and publishers wish to express their thanks to the below sources of illustrative material and/or permission to reproduce it. Some locations of artworks are also given below, in the interest of brevity:

From J. David Archibald, *Charles Darwin: A Reference Guide to His Life and Works* (Lanham, MD, 2019): p. 42; from Richard Beck, *A Treatise on the Construction, Proper Use, and Capabilities of Smith, Beck, and Beck's Achromatic Microscopes* (London, 1865), photo Wellcome Library, London: p. 101; Brooklyn Museum, NY (CC BY 3.0): p. 17; from Charles Darwin, *Insectivorous Plants* (New York, 1875), photo Princeton Theological Seminary Library, NJ: p. 173; from Charles Darwin, *Journal of Researches into the Natural History & Geology . . .* (London, 1913), photos Smithsonian Libraries, Washington, DC: pp. 44, 49, 62; from Francis Darwin, ed., *The Foundations of the Origin of Species: Two Essays Written in 1842 and 1844 by Charles Darwin* (Cambridge, 1909): p. 116 (left); from Francis Darwin, ed., *The Life and Letters of Charles Darwin, Including an Autobiographical Chapter*, vol. I (New York, 1898), photo NC State University Libraries, Raleigh: p. 57; Down House, Downe: p. 83 (right); photo eikira/Pixabay: p. 189 (top); The Fitzwilliam Museum, University of Cambridge: p. 18; from John Gilbert, illus., *The Crystal Palace that Fox Built: A Pyramid of Rhyme* (London, 1851), photo Getty Research Institute, Los Angeles, CA: p. 106; from John Gould, *Birds*, part III of Charles Darwin, ed., *The Zoology of the Voyage of HMS 'Beagle' . . .* (London, 1841), photo Library of Congress, Rare Book and Special Collections Division, Washington, DC: p. 55 (top); from *The Graphic*, XXXI/812 (20 June 1885): p. 189 (bottom); from H. N. Hutchinson, *Extinct Monsters: A Popular Account of Some of the Larger Forms of Ancient Animal Life* (New York, 1893), photo Smithsonian Libraries, Washington, DC: p. 48; from H. E. Litchfield, *Emma Darwin, Wife of Charles Darwin: A Century of Family Letters*, vol. II (Cambridge, 1904): pp. 116 (right), 184; from

Order of the Proceedings at the Darwin Celebration Held at Cambridge, June 22–June 24, 1909: With a Sketch of Darwin's Life (Cambridge, 1909), photos Wellcome Library, London: pp. 12, 19, 88, 91; from Eduard Pechuël-Loesche, *Brehms Tierleben: Allgemeine Kunde des Tierreichs* (Leipzig and Vienna, 1892), photos Smithsonian Libraries, Washington, DC: pp. 55 (bottom, vol. VI), 60 (vol. VII); from *Penny Magazine of the Society for the Diffusion of Useful Knowledge*, VII/375 (3 February 1838): p. 75; from *Popular Science Monthly*, vol. X (New York, 1877): p. 81; from *Popular Science Monthly*, vol. LXXIV (New York, 1909): p. 6; private collection: p. 83 (left); from *Punch; or, The London Charivari*, vol. LXXXI (22 October 1881): p. 181; from James Samuelson and William Crookes, eds, *Quarterly Journal of Science*, IV (London, 1867), photo Smithsonian Libraries, Washington, DC: p. 158 (right); courtesy Science History Institute, Philadelphia, PA: p. 16; reproduced by kind permission of the Syndics of Cambridge University Library: pp. 34 (MS DAR 204: 29), 69 (MS DAR 121, p. 36); from *Transactions of the Shropshire Archaeological Society and Natural History Society*, vol. VIII (Shrewsbury, 1885): pp. 22, 170; photo © The University of Edinburgh (CC BY 3.0): p. 26; from George R. Waterhouse, *Mammalia*, part II of Charles Darwin, ed., *The Zoology of the Voyage of HMS 'Beagle'* . . . (London, 1839), photo Library of Congress, Rare Book and Special Collections Division, Washington, DC: p. 51; The Wedgwood Museum, Barlaston: p. 40; Wellcome Collection, London (CC BY 4.0): pp. 13, 14, 32, 35, 39, 73, 74, 79, 89, 115, 128, 137, 158 (left), 168, 187.